D1446636

MAHARSHA
ON AGGADOS
אגדות מהרש"א

Selected Portions

Translated by
Rabbi Avraham Yaakov Finkel

YESHIVATH BETH MOSHE
SCRANTON, PA.

TABLE OF CONTENTS
BRACHOS, SHABBOS, ERUVIN

הקדמה
מראש הישיבה
מורינו הרב יעקב שניידמאן שליט"א

ידוע דאגדות חז"ל כוללים בתוכם סודות האמונה, וז"ל
הרמח"ל במאמר ההגדות ענין הגדות חז"ל למיניהם המאמרים
בהגדות יתחלקו לב' מינים, הא' כלל המאמרים הלימודיים, והב'
הביאורים. הלימודיים, הם המאמרים אשר יגידו בם עיקרים מעיקרי
החכמה, מוסרית או אלקית. וכו' והנה כבר ידעת שמה שהביא
לחז"ל לכתוב דברי התורה שבעל פה אחר היות המקובל אצלם
שדברים שבעל פה אסור ללמדם בכתב, היה מה שראו שהיו
הדיעות הולכות ומתחלשות באורך הגלות וחליפות הזמנים,
והזכרון מתמעט והסברא מתקצרת, ונמצאת התורה משתכחת. על
כן בחרו משום עת לעשות לה', לחקוק בספר פירוש המצות כלו,
למען ישאר קיים כל הימים, והוא כלל המשנה והגמרא. והנה
התבוננו עוד וראו שבחששא זאת שחששו על חלק המצות ראוי
היה לחוש גם כן על חלק סתרי התורה ועיקרי האלקיות וכו' אך
חלק הסודות אין ראוי שימסר כך לפני כל הרוצה ליטול את השם,
וכו' על כן גמרו לבצוע את הדין, והיינו לכתוב אותם, למען לא
יאבדו מן הדורות האחרונים, אך בדרכים נעלמים ומיני חידות שלא
יוכל לעמוד עליהם אלא מי שמסרו לו המפתחות, דהיינו הכללים
שבהם יובנו הרמזים ויפורשו החידות ההם, וכו' עכ"ל ולכאו' לפי
ביאור הרמח"ל יש לשאול, דביאורי המהרש"א על אגדות חז"ל
מגלים הרבה ענינים מסודות האמונה אשר הראשונים סתמום
מטעם שאמר הרמח"ל, ונמצא דספרו סותר כוונת חז"ל להסתיר
הסודות שנכללים בתוכם. וכמו כן יש לשאול על באר הגולה
למהר"ל מפראג ושאר מחברים שגילו פנימיות האגדות.

ונראה שיש בזה תרי טעמים חדא דמחברים האחרונים ראו
שיש ענין של עת לעשות הפרו תורותיך לגלות פנימיות האגדות,
כמו שחז"ל התירו לכתוב תורה שבע"פ. וביאורו דודאי מתחלה
הסתירו הענינים הפנימים, דחששו שיבוא מי שהוא וישתמש
בהענינים לדרכים של חולין, ולעשות מהם קרדום לעצמם. ובסודות

התורה יש לחוש ביותר שמי שישתמש בחכמה זו לדברי חולין יהיה
בזה חילול השם ומשו"ה הסתירו העניינים. אבל לאחר זמן רב של
אריכות הגלות וגם הלחץ הגדול להשתמד. ראו שסתימת העניינם
יגרום חלישות באמונת חז"ל אצל ההמון עם, בראותם עניינים זרים
בדברי חז"ל אשר אין להם ביאור, ויבואו ללעוג על כל מאמרי
חז"ל. ולא יאמרו שמחמת חסרון הבנתם נראים כעניינים זרים, וגם
ח"ו ילעגו על גופי הלכות שלמדו חז"ל מדרשת התורה.

עוד נראה טעם אחר דידוע דבזמן אחרית הימים יש הבטחה
שהקב"ה יגלה לנו סודות האמונה, והוא בכלל ההכנה לימות
משיח. וזהו הטעם דבזמנינו היה התגלות כתבי הזהר וגם הופיע
האר"י זצוק"ל, דגילה עניינים שהיו נסתרים מימות רשב"י והחברייא
הקדישא. ובגלל זה ראו האחרונים שיש לפרש עניני חז"ל דהם
פתח לידיעת סודות האמונה. דבאמת הוא בכלל השגחת הי"ת
לגלות אלו העניינים, וכמו שהקב"ה שלח לנו האר"י זצוק"ל כן שלח
לנו צדיקים וקדושים אחרים שפירשו לנו דברי חז"ל. דלאו הכל
ראוי לקבל העניינים על דרך קבלת האר"י זצוק"ל דהוא דרך
עמוקה והיה צורך לפרשם על דרך שיותר ראוי לכל ההמון.
והמהרש"א בביאורו על האגדות כולל בדבריו הרבה עניינים
יסודיים מסודות האמונה. ושמעתי שעיקר כוונתו היה רק לעשות
חיבור על האגדות, שראה שהוא דבר נחוץ כדי לחזק האמונה
והבטחון. והי"ת יסייענו ללמוד ולהבין דבריו על בורים.

SUMMARY OF
RABBI YAAKOV SCHNAIDMAN'S
PROLOGUE

It is known that the Aggadic portions of the Gemara contain the principles of faith. The Ramchal writes: "There are two types of Aggada. One deals with the explanation of various verses and teachings, and the other teaches fundamental principles of knowledge, of both ethical conduct and the knowledge of G-d.

"Although it was forbidden to write the Oral Torah, our Sages did write it down when they saw the intellectual capacity of the people diminishing with the prolonged exile and passage of time. Because people began to forget, and the Torah would have been forgotten, our sages followed the rule that one may act in ways which would otherwise be a desecration of the Torah, when something must be done in honor of G-d. Thus, our Sages permitted us to write the Mishnah and Gemara which is the explanation of all the mitzvos in order that they be remembered at all times.

"The Sages were also concerned that the mystical secrets and the fundamentals of G-dliness would be forgotten, however they did not want to make this portion accessible to whomever wanted to avail himself of this knowledge. Therefore, although they wrote it down so it would not be lost to the later generations, they couched the ideas in hidden ways and riddles so it would not be understood by those who did not posses the rules which are the keys to understanding them."

Based on this explanation, why did the Maharsha (in his work on Aggada), as well as the Maharal (in his work Be'er Ha'golah)

Rabbi Yaakov Schnaidman is the Rosh Yeshivah of Yeshivath Beth Moshe — Scranton, Pennsylvania.

and others who wrote on Aggada, reveal many of the secrets of faith which the earlier Sages had hidden?

Although the earlier sages saw fit to hide this knowledge so no one could use it for secular purposes which would bring about a desecration of G-d's name, however after the lengthy exile with the pressures for Jews to abandon their belief, the later sages felt that keeping these ideas secret would cause people to weaken their faith in the Sages. The common folk seeing strange things in the Aggada, would not base this on their lack of understanding, rather they might ridicule the words of the sages, eventually ridiculing even the laws of the Torah.

Secondly, we have a tradition that in the end of days, as a preparation for the coming of Mashiach, Hashem will reveal the secrets of faith. Thus the Zohar was found in our days, and the Ariz"l revealed many secrets which were hidden from the times of Rabbi Shimon bar Yochai and his holy group. Therefore the later authorities, including the Maharsha - realizing that not everyone can understand the esoteric tradition of the Ariz"l—explained the secrets of faith found in the Aggadic portions of the sages in a way that can be understood by all.

I heard that the Maharsha's primary goal was to write on the Aggada portions, in order to strengthen faith and trust in Hashem. May Hashem help us, to learn and understand his words properly.

TRANSLATOR'S INTRODUCTION

Chiddushei Aggados Maharsha is the monumental commentary on the *aggados* of the Talmud by Rabbi Shmuel Eliezer Eidels, known as the Maharsha.

Aggadah comprises the ethical and inspirational teachings of the Talmud, which contain a kaleidoscopic variety of inspiring tales, colorful parables and homilies that touch the soul and fire the imagination. The *aggados* are a window to a higher world; they elevate and uplift you. The word *aggadah*, derived from *aggeid*, "to bind, to draw," reflects the power of *aggadah* to draw one closer to Hashem. The Midrash sums it up concisely, "If you want to appreciate the greatness of the Creator, study *aggadah*, for through it you will get to know Him and cling to His ways" (*Sifrei, Eikev* 49).

The vast mosaic of *aggadah* can be divided into three major categories: (1) homiletical interpretations of Scriptural verses, (2) ethical teachings and descriptions of historical events, and (3) *aggados* dealing with metaphysical and mystical concepts.

The esoteric *aggados* are couched in cryptic parables, symbolisms, and metaphors concealing the true inner intent of the *aggados* beneath layer upon layer of allegory and allusion.

Rabbi Moshe Chaim Luzzatto (the Ramchal), in his Discourse on *Aggadah*, explains that the Sages conveyed these *aggados* in vague, figurative language because the secrets of the higher world and the mysteries of Heaven are not meant for the masses. If these teachings were formulated in plain language, evil-minded people might distort them to suit their nefarious purposes. In order to protect and preserve this knowledge for posterity, the Gemara phrased the *aggados* in allegorical wording whose true meaning was transmitted from master to disciple, so that only G-d-fearing Torah scholars would have the key to their meaning, while pseudo-scholars who do not have this key stumble about in the dark.

In his classic commentary *Chiddushei Aggados*, Maharsha ana-

lyzes and interprets the symbolism of the *aggados* and sheds light
on baffling anecdotes.

The Maharsha's major work is *Chiddushei Halachos*, a compre-
hensive commentary on the halachic part of the Talmud which became one of the most celebrated works in Torah literature. He pre-
sents an in-depth analysis of the Gemara and the commentaries of
Rashi and Tosafos, offering the student of Gemara an indispensable
tool for gaining a clear understanding of the *sugya* (subject matter)
at hand. The two commentaries were merged into *Chiddushei
Halachos VeAggados Maharsha* which is printed in all standard edi-
tions of the Talmud. The extreme brevity of his style often makes
it difficult to follow his reasoning. He habitually closes his remarks
with "*vekal lehavin*"—"this is easy to understand [and needs no
further elaboration]," while the topic is not simple at all. In fact,
the *Acharonim* (later authorities) spend a great deal of effort ana-
lyzing the latent meaning of *Maharsha*'s comments.

Rabbi Shmuel Eliezer Eidels (Maharsha) was born in Cracow,
Poland, 1555; he died in Ostroh, Poland in 1632. As a young man
he studied in Posen, Poland, where he married the daughter of
Rabbi Moshe Ashkenazi Heilprin. He founded a large yeshivah,
which was supported for twenty years by his mother-in-law, Eidel.
Because of that he was called by her name, Rav Shmuel Eidels.

The present volume offers a translation of selections of the
Maharsha's commentaries on the *aggados* in *maseches Berachos,
Shabbos* and *Eiruvin*. It is my hope that these insights will give you
an inkling of the eminence of this towering Torah scholar, inspiring you to greater dedication to Torah and mitzvos. *Zechuso yagein
aleinu*, May his merit protect us!

Avraham Yaakov Finkel
Sivan, 5767

Mesechta Brachos

THE THREE NIGHT WATCHES

⸺≋⊚≋⸺

BRACHOS 3a

GEMARA: R. Eliezer says: The night is divided into three [heavenly] watches . . . On earth, one can differentiate between these watches by the following signs: Donkeys bray, during the first watch; dogs bark during the second; a baby nurses from its mother's breasts, and a wife talks with her husband during the third.

Although these [three] signs must be understood in their literal sense, they also refer figuratively to the three levels of the soul, which the Kabbalists call, *nefesh, ruach* and *neshama.*

Nefesh is the lower soul, the physical life force which [controls man's behavior and actions. Man and animals share this soul.]

Ruach is the spirit which relates to emotions

Neshamah pertains to the mind.

Every action one does, is triggered by a corresponding level of the soul. Accordingly, man's activities during the night fall into three phases:

In the evening, man comes home exhausted after a day of strenuous work, his personality dominated by his *nefesh*, his earthly life force. Therefore, Rabbi Eliezer associates the first nightwatch with a braying donkey, [which personifies physicality, because the Hebrew word for donkey is *chamor*, which also means physicality].

In the middle of the night, a sleeping person is kept alive by his *ruach*, his spirit, as it says, *Into Your hand I entrust my spirit* (Tehillim 31:6). At this time, in the dark of night, demons and harmful spirits are released to wreak havoc on the world. This is what happened during the tenth plague, when the firstborn of the Egyptians died at midnight.

Keeping this in mind, R. Eliezer characterizes the second night-watch with barking dogs, for the Gemara says: When the Angel of Death comes to town, dogs howl (Bava Kamma 60b). [The death of the firstborn took place in the middle of the night. Naturally the dogs would have barked, however Hashem commanded them not to,] as it says, *But against B'nei Yisrael no dog shall bark* (Shemos 11:7).

In the third watch [at the end of the night,] man's sleep is over. Rested and relaxed with a clear mind, he is ready to engage in Torah study and *tefillah* which are functions of man's *neshamah*, the source of his intellect. Thus R. Eliezer describes the third watch as the time when "the baby nurses from its mother's breast." Metaphorically, "the mother's breast" represents the Torah, as the Gemara expounds the verse, *Her breasts will satisfy you at all times* (Mishlei 5:19). Why are the words of the Torah compared to a breast? Just as a child is succored whenever he sucks from a breast, so too, as often as a man studies Torah he relishes it (Eiruvin 54b).

Also during the third watch, a wife talks with her husband. In a figurative sense the wife exemplifies the Jewish community, prayerfully asking her husband—the Holy One, blessed be He—to fill her needs.

Three Kinds of Dreams

Similarly we can explain the Gemara which states: There are three kinds of dreams—one originates through an angel, another through a demon, and a third is prompted by the thoughts one had during the day (Berachos 55b).

A dream originating through an angel is triggered during the last watch, early in the morning, when one's mind is rested and clear. This dream is true. A dream caused by a demon starts in the second watch when demons and harmful spirits are given power to cause trouble, as mentioned above. A dream prompted by the thoughts one had during the day originates in the first watch, when a man's mind is occupied with the problems and challenges he encountered during the course of his day.

RECITING *ASHREI*

BRACHOS 4b

GEMARA: R. Elazar b. Avina said: Whoever recites the psalm, *Tehillah LeDavid*, "A praise by David" (Tehillim 145)[1] three times a day[2], can be confident that he is destined for the World to Come.

There is an opinion in the Gemara that we say [*Ashrei*] because the verses are arranged according to the *alef beis*, representing the Torah which was given with twenty two letters. However the Gemara rejects this, because Tehillim 119, *Happy are those whose ways are blameless*, is also arranged in alphabetical order; indeed it has eight verses for each letter of the *alef beis*.

Perhaps *Ashrei* is special because it contains the verse, *You open Your hand and satisfy the desire of every living thing* (Tehillim 145:16), and sustenance of every creature attests to G-d's continuous boundless benevolence. Additionally, the preceding verse, *The eyes of all, look to you with hope, and You give them their food in its proper time* (145:15), expresses the same praise of G-d. [But if so,] why not recite the Great Hallel (Tehillim 136), which lists all the kindnesses G-d bestowed on Yisrael, including, *He gives nourishment to all flesh, for His kindness endures forever* (136:25)?

The Gemara concludes that *Ashrei* contains both essentials, [the alphabetical order and G-d's sustenance of life]. The *aleph beis*, represents the Torah which is food for the soul, and sustenance, is food for the body. Both are necessary as it says, "If there is no flour there is no Torah; if there is no Torah, there is no flour" (Avos 3:21). [The body must be nourished in order to study. However, amassing worldly goods alone is not enough; man's mind must also be nourished with Torah.]

---

1   The psalm we refer to as "*Ashrei*."
2   We recite *Ashrei* twice during *Shacharis* and once at *Minchah*.

The Missing Letter *Nun*

BRACHOS 4b

GEMARA: Rabbi Yochanan said: Why isn't there a verse in *Ashrei* beginning with the letter *nun*?[3] Because a verse beginning with a *nun* predicts something dark for Yisrael, as it says, *"Naf'lah"— She has fallen—never to rise again, the maiden of Yisrael* (Amos 5:2).

By omitting [the verse beginning with the letter *nun*] which points to the downfall of Yisrael, David teaches that Yisrael's downfall is not final; rather, Yisrael will rise again, as the Gemara continues:

In Eretz Yisrael they translated the verse differently, [turning the curse into a blessing:] They read: *She has fallen, never to [fall gain.] Arise, O maiden of Yisrael!*

R. Nachman b. Yitzchak says that this idea is apparent in the verse itself, for in the next verse David lent support to Yisrael through his *ruach hakodesh,* saying *G-d supports all that have fallen* (145:14)

For although Yisrael would never rise again, were she to be judged on her own merits, *G-d supports all those who have fallen,* out of His abundant kindness, though they do not deserve His support.

---

[3]   *Ashrei* is arranged alphabetically, however there is no verse beginning with the letter *nun*.

THE ANGELS MICHAEL AND GAVRIEL

══•◉•══

BRACHOS 4b

GEMARA: R. Elazar b. Avima said: What was said about [the angel] Michael is greater than what was said about [the angel] Gavriel. About Michael it says, *Then, one of the serafim flew to me* (Yeshayah 6:6) [in a non-stop flight] whereas about Gavriel it says, *The man Gavriel, whom I had previously seen in the vision, was lifted in flight* (Daniel 9:21). [The implication is that Gavriel must pause midway in his flight]. We learn: Michael in one flight, Gavriel in two flights, Eliyahu in four flights, the Angel of Death in eight flights, and during an epidemic in one flight.

The underlying thought is this: Michael [the guardian angel of Yisrael] is symbolized by water. Standing on the right side [of the Divine Chariot],[4] he represents the attribute of compassion. The angel Gavriel is symbolized by fire. Standing to the left, he administers justice.[5] Since G-d's compassion is very great, Michael is empowered to carry out his mission [of compassion] in one flight [without stopping]. Gavriel must pause when carrying out his mission [of strict justice], to give the sinner time to repent. G-d will then relent, as happened in the city of Nineveh (Yonah 3:5-10).

Eliyahu who was created from all four elements, water, fire, air and earth, carried out his mission in four flights with three intermediary stops. This was evident in the case of the child of the

---

4   In Kabbalah literature, Michael represents the *sefirah* of *Chesed* (Kindness) which represents water, silver, and the right side (*Zohar* vol.1, 98b,99a; *sisrei Torah* vol.2, 147a).

5   In Kabbalah literature Gavriel represents the *Sefirah* of *Gevurah* (Power).

woman of Tzorfas, as it says, *He stretched himself out over the boy three times* (1 Melachim 17:21).

The Angel of Death needs eight flights to carry out his mission, making seven intermediary stops, in the hope that meanwhile the person will repent. For this reason we stop seven times during a funeral.

The Mitzvah of *Kerias HaTorah*

BRACHOS 5a

GEMARA: R. Levi bar Chama said: What is the meaning of the verse, *I will give you the stone tablets, the Torah and the commandments that I have written for [the people's] instruction* (Shemos 24:12)? . . . *the Torah*—refers to that which is read, meaning Scripture.

Since tractate *Berachos* is the first *mesechta* of the Talmud, the Gemara states that the Torah is called *mikra*, "that which is read," because it is a mitzvah to read the Torah from a hand-written scroll, articulating the words with their vowels and cantillation marks. This is not necessary when learning Mishnah and Gemara.

Three Precious Gifts

BRACHOS 5a

GEMARA: The Holy One, blessed be He, gave Yisrael three precious gifts, and all of them are obtained only through suffering. They are: The Torah, Eretz Yisrael, and the World to Come.

[T]orah is a precious gift,] as it says, *For I have given you a good teaching, do not forsake My Torah* (Mishlei 4:2). Eretz Yisrael is a precious gift, as it says, *For the good land that He has given you* (Devarim 8:10). The World to Come is a precious gift, as it says, *See, I have placed before you today the life and the good* (Devarim 30:15).

Torah is obtained through suffering, because indulging in the delights of this world leads to neglect of Torah study. As it says: This is the way of the Torah: Eat bread with salt, drink water in small measure, sleep on the ground, and live a life of deprivation— but toil in the Torah (Avos 6:4).

Eretz Yisrael is obtained through suffering, teaching us that we were not given Eretz Yisrael in order to enjoy its fruits and revel in the good things [it has to offer], because [self-indulgence] leads to defiance of G-d, as it says, *You may then eat and be satisfied . . . But your heart may then grow haughty, and you may forget Hashem your G-d* (Devarim 8:12,14).

The World to Come is obtained through suffering in this world, which erases one's sins, allowing him to receive his full reward in the World to Come.

Our Sages required us to mention *b'ris,* Torah, Eretz Yisrael, life of the World to Come and Kingship of the House of David in [the berachos of] *Birkas Hamazon* (Berachos 48b). This teaches us not to overindulge in delicacies; rather one should eat only his fill, thereby remembering *bris*—that He made a covenant with us—to acquire Torah, Eretz Yisrael, and life in the World to Come through suffering.

In *parashas Eikev* suffering and affliction are mentioned three times, corresponding to these gifts.

1. *The entire commandment that I command you today* (Devarim 8:1), referring to Torah study which is equivalent to all the mitzvos, is followed by, *in order to afflict you, to test you* (8:2).

2. *Just as a man chastises his son, so is Hashem your G-d chastising you* (Devarim 8:5), is followed by, *Hashem your G-d is bringing you to a good land* (8:7), teaching that Eretz Yisrael is acquired through suffering.

3. *He sent hardships to test you, to do good to you in the end* (8:16), *the end* refers to the World to Come, teaching that the World to Come is acquired through suffering.

A Rejected Prayer

BRACHOS 5b

GEMARA: If two people entered to pray, and one finished praying and left, not waiting for his fellow to finish, his prayer is tossed aside in front of him.

Angels of mercy bring a person's prayer before G-d. However, if one is undeserving his prayer is cast aside by accusing angels, preventing it from reaching G-d. [When one leaves before his fellow finishes] he disrupts his fellow's concentration [because he worries about being left alone. Therefore,] his prayer is rejected measure for measure.

Study Partners

BRACHOS 6a

GEMARA: [When two people learn Torah together] their words are inscribed in the "Book of Remembrance."

When two people learn Torah together, through their discussion they generally arrive at a true understanding of the subject matter, thus their words deserve to be written in G-d's "Book of Remembrance." One who learns alone may err; therefore, his words do not merit to be recorded in this book.

SHARED LOVE AND DEVOTION

BRACHOS 6a

GEMARA: How do you know that the Holy One, blessed be He, puts on tefillin? Because it says, *G-d has sworn by His right hand and by the strength of His arm* (Yeshayah 62:8).

The mitzvah of tefillin signifies that we are close to Hashem, dedicated to Him with our heart, our soul, and our resources. When we wear tefillin the *Shechinah* hovers over us. In the same way, Hashem is attached to us, as it says, *I am my Beloved's, and my Beloved is mine* (Shir Hashirim 6:3).

Just as Yisrael takes pride in G-d, so does G-d take pride in Yisrael as is expressed in the two verses, *Today you have granted praise and importance to Hashem*, and, *Hashem has granted praise and importance to you* (Devarim 26:17,18). [Just as Yisrael wears tefillin which contain praises of G-d, so does G-d wear tefillin which contain verses that praise Yisrael]. That is why tefillin are called *pe'er*—glory, for G-d wears tefillin to attach Himself to His nation Yisrael and glorify them. And so Yisrael says, *For the sake of my love, place me like a seal on Your heart* (Shir Hashirim 8:6), meaning that G-d is as close to us as arm-tefillin which are worn on the left arm, opposite the heart.

MOSHE IS REWARDED MEASURE FOR MEASURE

———◈———

BRACHOS 7a

GEMARA: [When Moshe had the vision at the
burning bush, *he hid his face, for he was afraid to
gaze toward G-d* (Shemos 3:6).] In reward for
three things [that Moshe did at the burning bush]
he merited three things. In reward for *Moshe hid
his face*, he merited the shining face;[6] in reward for
for he was afraid, he merited *and they feared to approach him*[7]. In reward for *to gaze*, he merited *He
beholds the likeness of Hashem* (Bamidbar 12:8).

When one attempts to comprehend metaphysical concepts
he must be fearful for three reasons:

1. A person is afraid to approach a grand and awe-inspiring
sight. [And so Iyov said,] *Youths would see me and conceal themselves*
(Iyov 29:8). This is a rational fear.

2. Recognizing his limited intelligence, a person is unwilling to
reflect on an obscure and abstract concept for fear of reaching a
wrong conclusion. This is also a rational fear.

3. One fears the esoteric nature of a subject, which is beyond
human comprehension.

Moshe was afraid for all of these above reasons:

1. *He was afraid* refers to the rational fear he had of the grand
and incomprehensible thing he saw, [i.e., the vision of the burning
bush].

---

[6] When Moshe came down from Mount Sinai with the two Tablets, the skin of his
face had become radiant (*Shemos* 34:29).
[7] When Aharon and B'nei Yisrael saw his radiant face, *They were afraid to approach
him* (*Shemos* 34:30).

2. He realized that his intellect was not capable [of grasping the meaning of the vision of the burning bush] so he *hid his face*. One's intellectual capacity is referred to as one's face; hiding one's face shows that one feels intellectually incapable of comprehending the subject.

3. He was afraid *to gaze toward G-d* (Shemos 3:6), refers to his fear of the esoteric nature of the vision [of the burning bush] which by its very nature was incomprehensible to man.

Because of this he was rewarded, measure for measure:

Moshe hid his face—Because he thought his intellectual capacity was inadequate, he merited that his face became radiant, and he was granted the ability to understand the most profound concepts.

Because *he was afraid*, [of the grand thing he saw], he merited that, *they feared to approach him*. They were afraid of him because of his lofty spiritual stature.

Because he feared he would not comprehend the esoteric nature of the subject represented by the words, *to gaze*, he merited that, *He beholds the likeness of Hashem*. Moshe was granted the ability to comprehend G-d as much as humanly possible—this is called a vision of the Back, as Rashi explains the verse, "*You will see My back, however My Face will not be seen*", *My face* refers to the essence of G-d, which is not humanly comprehensible, as it says, *No human can see My face and live* (Shemos 33:20). . .

THE IMPORTANCE OF GOING TO *SHUL*

———◉———

BRACHOS 8a

GEMARA: Whoever has a synagogue in his city but does not go there to pray is called a bad neighbor, for it says, *As for My wicked neighbors who damage the inheritance that I gave to My people Yisrael* (Yirmeyah 12:14).

[T]he inheritance that I gave to My people Yisroel, refers to Eretz Yisroel, however it is applied to a synagogue] based on this Gemara: In time to come [with the coming of Mashiach] all synagogues and study halls outside of Eretz Yisrael will be transplanted to Eretz Yisrael (Megillah 29a). [Since synagogues will become part of Eretz Yisrael] the inheritance that G-d gave to Yisroel, one who neglects going to *shul* damages Eretz Yisrael.

[In connection with this, the Gemara cites the following dialogue:] They said to R. Yochanan: "There are elderly people in Babylonia." R. Yochanan questioned: "[How can this be?] Regarding Eretz Yisroel it says, *In order to prolong your days and the days of your children on the land that Hashem has sworn to give to them*, however there is no promise of longevity outside Eretz Yisrael!

Then they told R. Yochanan that the aged of Babylonia arise early to go *shul* in the morning and stay late in the evening. He responded: "In that merit they gained long life." [The Maharsha explains:] Since the synagogues of Babylonia will be moved to Eretz Yisrael, they are already considered part of Eretz Yisrael, and one who visits a synagogue merits longevity like one who dwells in Eretz Yisrael.

The Gemara brings support from the verse: *Happy is the man who listens to Me, who comes quickly to My doors day by day, to guard the doorposts of My entrance ways* (Mishlei 8:34). [The Maharsha explains:] The repetitive *day by day* implies that they get up early every morning to go to *shul*. *To guard the doorposts of My entrance* suggests that they go to *shul* at night like a watchman who guards the study hall at night.

The verse continues: *For he who finds Me finds life* (Mishlei 8:35). [Explains the Maharsha:] Since G-d is found in the synagogue, he who spends time in the synagogue will live long.

The Blessing Before Learning Torah

———— ⸎ ————

BRACHOS 11b

GEMARA: What berachah does one recite [before learning Torah]? R. Yehudah said: "Who has sanctified us . . . and has commanded us *la'asok bedivrei Torah*—to involve ourselves with words of Torah." R. Yochanan concludes this berachah with *"veha'arev na*—sweeten the words of Your Torah in our mouths." R. Hamenuna said: [The berachah as follows:] *"Asher bachar banu mikol ha'amim . . .*—Who selected us from all the nations . . ."

There are three reasons why a person does something: (1) because it is good; (2) because it is pleasing; and (3) because it is beneficial.

Therefore, we begin by saying the berachah: *"la'asok bedivrei Torah*—to involve ourselves with the words of Torah," for nothing is as *good* as Torah study. It elevates us to the level of angels, which is the ultimate *good*.

Next we say the berachah of *"veha'arev na*—sweeten the words of Your Torah in our mouths," for nothing is as *pleasing* and sweet as Torah study, as it says, *[The Torah is] sweeter than honey* (Tehillim 19:11)

Then we say the berachah *"Asher bachar banu mikol ha'amim*— Who selected us from all the nations"—for the Torah is *beneficial* in helping us resist the nations, and in setting us apart from them. For this reason, R. Hamenuna says that this berachah is the most beneficial of the berachos.

We say all three berachos, for they encompass the three qualities of the Torah: *good, pleasing,* and *beneficial.*

THE ORDER OF THE SECTIONS OF THE *SHEMA*

BRACHOS 13a

> GEMARA: Why does the portion of *Vehayah im shamo'a* precede *Vayomer*? Because [the mitzvah of learning Torah which is mentioned in] *Vehayah im shamo'a* applies by day and by night, [whereas the mitzvah of tzitzis which is the subject of] *Vayomer*, applies only by day.

V*ayomer* is in *parashas Shelach* (Bamidbar 15:37-41); *Vehayah im shamo'a* is in *parashas Eikev*. (Devarim 11:13-21)] Since both these portions deal with the acceptance of G-d's absolute sovereignty, why are they not recited in the order they appear in the Torah [*Vayomer* before *Vehayah im shamo'a*]? Addressing these questions, the Gemara gives the above mentioned answer.

Another reason [for the order of the three *parshios* is:] The three *parshios* of the Shema declare the three fundamental principles of the Jewish faith, namely:

> The existence of G-d; the divinity of the Torah; and the concept of rewards and punishment.

The first portion of *Shema* contains our acceptance of G-d's sovereignty and is our explicit declaration of the existence of G-d and His Oneness.

This is followed by, *Vehayah im shamo'a tishme'u el mitzvosai* in which we express our acceptance of the mitzvos and affirm our belief that the mitzvos were given by G-d.

Finally comes *Vayomer*, which speaks of the reward for Yisrael and the punishment of the Egyptians.

PROLONGING THE WORD *ECHAD*

━━━━━●◉●━━━━━

BRACHOS 13b

GEMARA: We learnt in a Braisa, Sumchus says: "Whoever draws out the word *echad*—One, [in the phrase *Shema Yisrael Hashem Elokeinu Hashem echad*—Hear O Yisrael, Hashem is our G-d, Hashem is One,] will have his days and years extended. Rav Achah ben Yaakov says this refers to the letter *daled* [in the word *echad*.] Rav Ashi says: Nonetheless he should not rush when saying the *ches*.

R. Yirmeyah prolonged his pronunciation of the word *echad* a great deal. R. Chiya b. Abba said to him: Once you [mentally] acknowledged [G-d's] kingship [in heaven] above, [on earth] below, and over the four directions of the skies, no more is required.

Rabbeinu Yonah says one should prolong the *ches* of *echad* as long as it takes to acknowledge G-d's kingship in heaven and on earth. One should also stretch out the *daled* [which has the numeric value of four] to acknowledge G-d's kingship over the four directions of the sky. However, Rashi explains that [one should not prolong the *ches*], rather one should have both thoughts in mind when prolonging the *daled*. This seems to be the intent of the Gemara since Sumchus said one should draw out the *daled*.

R. Yirmeyah prolonged his pronunciation of the word *echad* longer than the time it takes to contemplate G-d's kingship above and below, in order to meditate on the Kabbalistic and esoteric meanings of this word. R. Chiya b. Abba warned him that by doing so he would fall behind the rest of the congregation, not reciting the *Shemoneh esrei* with them as required. He said: It is enough to contemplate that G-d is the sole Master, above, below, and in all four directions, which is all the general public can concentrate on. This is alluded to in the letters of the word *echad*, written: *alef, ches, daled*. The numeric value of *alef*—one—alludes to G-d who is One. That he is master in the seven heavens and on earth, corresponds to the numeric value of *ches*—eight. That He reigns over the four directions, corresponds to the numeric value of *daled*—four.

SHABBOS, MILAH, AND TEFILLIN

————◦◉◦————

BRACHOS 14b

GEMARA: Ulla said: If one recites the *Shema* without wearing tefillin, it is as if he uttered false testimony against himself.

According to Rashi, "himself" is used as a euphemism for G-d. In this chapter G-d commanded us to wear tefillin, so one who does not wear tefillin when saying this chapter denies G-d's commandments. Because the Gemara does not want to say [explicitly] that he utters false testimony against G-d, it says instead "against Himself." Rabbeinu Yonah translates the word "himself" literally, for one who says the paragraph containing the command to wear tefillin without actually wearing them testifies that he does not keep the commandments.

However, the commentators explain this based on the following: G-d gave us three mitzvos as a sign and testimony that we are His nation, namely: Shabbos, *milah*, and tefillin.

Concerning Shabbos it says, *Between Me and B'nei Yisrael it is a sign forever* (Shemos 31:16). About *milah* it says, *It shall be the sign of the covenant between Me and you* (Bereishis 7:11). Regarding tefillin it says, *Bind them as a sign on your arm and let them be tefillin between your eyes* (Devarim 6:8).

We know that, *A case must be established through the testimony of two witnesses* (Devarim 19:15). On Shabbos we need not put on tefillin, because we have two witnesses: Shabbos and Milah. But on weekdays the two necessary witnesses are, milah and tefillin. One who does not put on tefillin on a weekday, is lacking his second witness, thus it is as if he utters false testimony.

CONTEMPLATING G-D'S GREATNESS

———◦◉◦———

BRACHOS 17a

GEMARA: A favorite saying of R. Meir was: Learn with all your heart and all your soul to know My ways, and study Torah diligently and consistently . . .

Philosophers who delve into the knowledge of G-d, teach, that one is required to contemplate G-d's existence, His unity, His omnipotence, and His ways, to the extent of one's intellectual ability. If something seems to contradict the holy Torah, he should not follow his intellect, rather he should attribute it to his lack of understanding.

This is what R. Meir means to say: Learn with all your heart to understand G-d's ways. In His ways you will find proof of His existence, His unity, and His omnipotence. [Trying to understand these ideas] is very important. Even [a man as exalted as] Moshe Rabbeinu sought to fathom these concepts when he asked G-d, *Please let me have a vision of Your glory* (Shemos 33:18). However,

R. Meir added, and study Torah diligently and consistently, for when a thought that seems to contradict the Torah enters the mind of one who diligently and steadily learns Torah, he will know that it is a heretical idea, and dismiss it from his mind.

R. Yochanan's Humility

BRACHOS 28b

GEMARA: R. Yochanan b. Zakkai fell ill, and his disciples visited him. When he saw them, he began to cry. His disciples asked him: "Why do you cry?" He replied: "There are two paths before me, one leading to Gan Eden and the other to Gehinnom, and I do not know on which they will lead me; shall I not cry?"

At the moment of his passing he said to them: "Remove the utensils because of ritual impurity, and prepare a throne for Chizkiyahu the King of Yehudah who is coming [to escort me]."

I have seen explained that, the tzaddik, [R. Yochanan ben Zakkai] said this, because he did not believe in himself, as was the case with David, who said, *Had I not trusted that I would see the goodness of Hashem in the land of life [i.e., the World to Come]* (Tehillim 27:13). Perhaps he did not want to glorify himself in front of his disciples, thus teaching them a lesson in humility. Therefore he said: "Remove the utensils because of impurity," implying that he was about to die [like any human being]. Nevertheless, he told them King Chizkiyah was coming to escort him, so they should not suspect him of improper conduct.

THE *SHEMONEH ESREI*

━━•◦◉◦•━━

BRACHOS 28b

GEMARA: The eighteen berachos [of the Shemoneh Esrei] correspond to the eighteen times that David mentioned G-d's name in the psalm: *Render unto Hashem, you sons of the powerful* (Tehillim 29:1) . . . The seven berachos of the [Shemoneh Esrei] of Shabbos correspond to the seven times David mentioned the word "voice" [in Psalm 29, beginning with *The voice of Hashem is upon the waters.*] . . . The nine berachos [of the Shemoneh Esrei] of Rosh Hashanna correspond to the nine times G-d's Name is mentioned in the prayer of Channa (Shemuel I 2:1-10).

The weekday Shemoneh esrei has eighteen berachos, which is the numerical value of the word *chai*—life, because in the middle section which contains the majority of the berachos, one makes his personal pleas to Hashem. In Psalm 29 the four letter Name of Hashem representing His attribute of compassion, is mentioned eighteen times hinting to the eighteen berachos. All the berachos end with this Name as well. On weekdays, when we ask for our personal needs we appeal to G-d's compassion, petitioning Him in a low voice. [Therefore the berachos are hinted at without the word voice.] However, on Shabbos the seven berachos are recited to praise Hashem—not for our needs, so we may use a loud voice. [Therefore the berachos are hinted at using the word voice.] Rosh Hashanah, is a Day of Judgment, when we must pray for Hashem's mercy, therefore, the nine berachos of the Shemoneh esrei of Rosh Hashanah are also hinted to with the Name of mercy without the word voice, for it is forbidden to pray on Rosh Hashanna in a loud voice.

REMEMBER THE DAY OF DEATH

===◉===

BRACHOS 31a

GEMARA: At the wedding of Mar, Ravina's grand-
son, the rabbis said to R. Hammenuna Zuti:
"Please sing us a song!" He sang: "Woe is to us,
for we all will die! Woe is to us for we all will die!"
They asked: "What refrain shall we sing?" He
replied: "Where is the Torah, and where is the
mitzvah that will protect us [from the judgment
of Gehinnom!]".

Man should always be mindful of his death for two
reasons.

1. To ward off the evil inclination, as it says: One must constantly prod his *yetzer tov* to fight against his *yetzer hara*. If he sub-
dues it, fine. If not, he should remind himself of the day of death
(Berachos 5a).

2. To prod himself to repent, as it says: Repent one day before
your death. Since one might die tomorrow, he will spend his whole
life in *teshuvah* (Shabbos 153a).

[R. Hamenuna] said the phrase, "Woe is to us, for we all will
die!" twice, first to immobilize the *yetzer hara*; and then to prod us
to do *teshuvah*, for one might die the next day.

When they asked, "What refrain shall we sing"? He replied:
"Where is the Torah and where is the mitzvah" . . . [We need the
Torah] to subdue the *yetzer hara*, as it says: If one's evil inclination
overpowers him he must attempt to subdue it. If he is successful,
fine. If not, he should immerse himself in Torah learning. If he is
still unsuccessful he should remind himself of the day of death.

Mitzvos also help one do teshuvah, and protect us from death,
as it says, *This is your life the length of your days* (Devarim 30:20).

DO SINNERS HAVE A VALID EXCUSE?

━━●●◉●●━━

BRACHOS 32a

GEMARA: R. Chama B'Rabbi Chanina said: If not for these three verses [which imply that G-d could have removed the yetzer hara], the feet of Yisrael would have stumbled, [for G-d would be able to blame them completely for their sins.]

One verse is: *Whom I have caused to wrong* (Michah 4:6); the second, *Behold, as the clay in the potter's hand, so are you in My hand* (Yirmeyah 18:6); the third, *I will take away the stony heart out of your flesh, and I will give you a heart of flesh* (Yechezkel 36:26).

Rashi explains: [If not for these three verses] Yisrael would have no justification [for their sins] in the heavenly Court. But [these verses] give us an excuse [implying that G-d made us sin by giving us the *yetzer hara*.] However, this argument does not hold water, because man was given *bechirah* (free will), as the Gemara says: "I created the *yetzer hara*, but I also created the antidote for it—the Torah (Kiddushin 30b)." If man did not have freedom to choose [between good and evil], there would be no reward [for righteousness] nor punishment [for transgressing]. But man was given *bechirah* so he can earn merit by overcoming the *yetzer hara* and be rewarded on Judgment Day.

Rather, R. Chama means that a sinner can offer a slight justification [for his wrongdoing by arguing that] G-d created the *yetzer hara* which made him sin. [Therefore,] after being punished for his transgressions he will be acquitted, so he should not stumble completely in the heavenly Court and be destroyed.

[The Gemara says:] R. Elazar said: Eliyahu spoke defiantly

against G-d [saying it was G-d's fault that Yisrael worshipped idols, because He created the *yetzer hara*,] and G-d endorsed Eliyahu's statement (Berachos 31b). Here too, the meaning is that he agreed that they would not stumble completely, but be acquitted after punishment. R. Elazar says Eliyahu spoke "defiantly" against G-d, because his claim was not actually valid, for they were given free will, and should have conquered their *yetzer hara*.

TWO KINDS OF *YIR'AH*

BRACHOS 33b

GEMARA: R. Chanina said: Everything is in the hand of heaven except fear of heaven, as it says, *And now, Yisrael, what does Hashem your G-d want of you? Only that you fear Hashem* (Devarim 10:12). [Only that you fear Hashem, implies that fear of Heaven is easy to acquire. Asks the Gemara:] Is fear of heaven such a little thing? Has not R. Chanina said: G-d's treasury is filled with nothing but fear of heaven? [Answers the Gemara:] Yes, as far as Moshe is concerned it a small thing. This is illustrated with a parable: If a man is asked for a big article and he has it, it seems like a small article to him; if he is asked for a small article and he does not possess it, it seems like a big article to him.

Why did the Gemara respond to R. Chanina's statement with the question: "Is the fear of heaven such a little thing?" rather than asking this about the verse itself?

The parable is also difficult to understand. The parable says: "If a person is asked for a big article, and he has it, it seems like a small article to him. If he is asked for a small article, and he does not have it, it seems like a big article to him". The parable does not seem to fit the verse, because Moshe was telling Yisrael that fear of heaven was a small thing although they certainly agreed that *yir'ah*—fear of G-d—was a big thing!

There are two kinds of *yir'ah*:

1. Natural *yir'ah*, where one fears G-d because he is afraid of punishment [for disobedience]. This kind of fear is considered a little thing [because this is not a high level of fear].

2. Rational fear, where one is in awe of an imposing and amazing wonder. For example, *[After his dream, Yaakov] became frightened and said, "How awesome is this place! This is none other than the abode of G-d"* (Bereishis 28:17). This is the perfect form of *yir'ah*, the "big thing" [in the parable].

The simple interpretation of the verse, *only that you fear Hashem,* refers to fear of punishment, which is natural *yir'ah*, and is indeed a "little thing." However, when R. Chanina said: "Everything is in the hand of heaven except the fear of heaven", we assume that he had rational fear in mind, since this is not in the hands of heaven but arises from man's free will. By contrast, natural fear [of punishment] is partially in the hands of heaven, [for punishment is meted out by G-d] and people will naturally fear G-d when they see others being punished. As the Gemara says: "Calamity comes into the world because of Yisrael, to frighten them so they will do *teshuvah*, as it says, *I said, "Just fear Me, accept chastisement* (Tzefaniah 3:6) (Yevamos 63a).

R. Chanina when saying that G-d's treasury is filled with nothing but fear of heaven, is referring to rational *yir'ah* which derives from a person's free will, and is a precious item worthy of being stored in Hashem's treasury. This is not a little thing, for it says, *The beginning of wisdom is the fear of Hashem* (Tehillim 111:10). However, because he brings proof from the verse, *only that you fear Hashem,* apparently he interpreted this verse as referring to rational *yir'ah* and thereby deeming it a "little thing."

The Gemara answers that the phrase, *only that you fear Hashem,* does indeed refer to rational fear, however it is not "little" in importance. Rather, Moshe was easily able to inspire the people with rational fear, for they saw in him a wondrous and awesome phenomenon, namely that *the skin of his face had become luminous, and they were afraid to come close to him* (Shemos 34:29). They had no fear of being punished by Moshe, for he had no power to punish without Hashem's consent. Since their rational *yir'ah* of Moshe was as strong as their awe of Hashem, Moshe properly said, *What does Hashem your G-d want of you? Only that you fear Him,* just as you fear me with rational *yir'ah*. This is similar to R. Yochanan b. Zakkai saying "May it be the will of G-d that the [rational] fear of heaven be upon you like the [rational] fear [you have of a awesome person] of flesh and blood" (Berachos 28b). Thus we can explain the parable: If a man is asked for a big article—meaning rational fear, which ranks very high—since he must acquire it through his own free will, and he is in the company of awe inspiring people, it will seem like a small article to him. The one in the parable who was asked for a small article, is the one who does not even have natural inborn fear, which is partially in the hand of heaven, as we explained above. If he is not inspired by natural events he will not acquire it and it seems like a big article to him.

REWARD IN THE HEREAFTER

BRACHOS 34b

GEMARA: R. Chiya b. Abba said in the name of R. Yochanan: All the prophecies [of magnificent bounties that will be showered on Yisrael in the future] were directed to a person who marries off his daughter to a Torah scholar; to one who does business on behalf of a Torah scholar [enabling him to devote his time to Torah study]; and to one who shares some of his wealth with a Torah scholar. However for the Torah scholar himself, *No eye has seen it, O G-d, but You, who acts for those who trust in Him* (Yeshayah 64:3).

The three individuals mentioned in this Gemara correspond to the three non-Torah scholars mentioned in the Gemara on the verse, *And you who cleave to Hashem your G-d are all alive today* (Devarim 4:4). The Gemara asks, Is it possible to cleave to the Divine Presence? The Gemara answers, If one marries his daughter to a Torah scholar, does business with a Torah scholar, or sustains a Torah scholar from his own possessions, it is considered as if he cleaved to the Divine Presence (Kesubos 111b). He will receive all the magnificent earthly bounties which can be comprehended by a physical man. However the reward in store for a Torah scholar can only be given in the World to Come, for it is a spiritual reward unfathomable to the human mind. As it says, *No eye has seen it, O G-d, but You who acts for those who trust in Him* (Yeshayah 64:3), meaning Torah scholars.

The same is true for the next statement of R. Chiya b. Abba in the name of R. Yochanan: "The prophets prophesied only for the days of Mashiach, but they could not perceive the reward of the World to Come, as it says, *No eye has seen it, O G-d, but You.*"

Because [the dead] will rise in body and soul in the days of Mashiach, their reward will be physical, which can be seen by the prophets, but the spiritual reward of the World to Come cannot be perceived by the prophets, as it says, *No eye has seen it, O G-d, but You.*

This is also the underlying idea of the next statement by R. Chiya b. Abba in the name of R. Yochanan: "All the [glorious things] the prophets prophesied for the future, apply to *baalei teshuvah* [returnees to Torah]. But the perfectly righteous, will merit an indescribably great spiritual reward, *No eye has seen it, O G-d, but You.*"

Since the *baalei teshuvah* gave in to their physical drive, they will receive only a physical reward, but the perfectly righteous will merit an indescribably great spiritual reward, which *No eye has seen it, O G-d, but You.*

That the prophecy refers to, one who marries his daughter to a Torah scholar, the days of Mashiach, and *baalei teshuvah*, were all said by R. Chiya b. Abba in the name of R. Yochanan, therefore, these interpretations don't contradict one another. Thus, one who marries his daughter to a Torah scholar [but is himself not a Torah scholar] will be rewarded only with the reward mentioned in the Prophets even in the World to Come. The Torah scholar will only be rewarded [with spiritual reward] in the World to Come and not in the days of Mashiach. *Baalei teshuvah* will only be rewarded with the reward mentioned in the Prophets even in the World to Come.

THE GREATNESS OF A BAAL TESHUVAH

———— ❉ ————

BRACHOS 34b

> GEMARA: R. Abbahu said: In the place where baalei teshuvah stand, even the perfectly righteous cannot stand, as it says, *Peace, peace, for the far and the near* (Yeshayah 57:19). *The far*, which refers to one who sinned and was far from Hashem, is mentioned before *the near*, which refers to one who never sinned and was always near Hashem. However, R. Yochanan says: *Far*, refers to the perfect tzaddik, who was far from transgression from the beginning. *Near*, refers to the *baal teshuvah*, who once was near to transgression and now has gone far from it.

I t seems unreasonable, that baalei teshuvah are on a higher level that *tzaddikim*.

The commentators have proposed various explanations, and I will offer my own.

R. Yochanan, interpreted the word *near* to mean, one who was near transgression and now has gone far from it [and repented]. "Near transgression" does not mean a person who actually transgressed; it means one who intended to transgress but overcame his *yetzer hara* (evil impulse) and did not transgress. Ultimately he repented of his intention to transgress. R. Abuha was referring to this person when he said the *baal teshuvah* ranks higher than a perfect tzaddik who was never tempted by his *yetzer hara* and never came close to transgressing.

However R. Yochanan believes that a perfect *tzaddik* is on a higher level, for he did not transgress even in thought, as opposed to one who thought about transgressing.

COMBINING TORAH STUDY WITH
A WORLDLY OCCUPATION

BRACHOS 35b

GEMARA: Our Rabbis taught: What can we learn from the phrase, *You shall gather in your grain* (Devarim 11:14)? I might think the verse, *Let not this Book of the Torah cease from your lips* (Yehoshua 1:8), should be taken literally [and no one should engage in a worldly occupation]. Therefore it says, *You shall gather in your grain*, implying that one should combine the study of Torah with a worldly occupation. This is the view of R. Yishmael.

R. Shimon b. Yochai said: Is this possible? If a man plows in the plowing season, and plants in the planting season . . . what will become of the

Torah? [When will he have time to learn Torah?]
However when Yisrael does the will of G-d, their
work is performed by others, as it says, *Foreigners*
will stand and tend your flocks, and the sons of the
stranger will be your plowmen and your vineyard
workers (Yeshayah 59:5).

Abaye said: Many have followed the advice of
R. Yishmael [combining Torah study with a
worldly occupation], and it has worked well.
Others have followed R. Shimon b. Yochai and
have not been successful.

The Gemara can be explained as follows: Surely the work of
perfect tzaddikim will be done by others, but they are few in
number, as Rabbi Shimon b. Yochai said: I have seen saintly people
who behold the *Shechinah*, but they are few. If there are a thou-
sand, my son and I are among them; if there are a hundred, my son
and I are among them, and if there are only two, they are my son
and I (Sukkah 45b). Since there are so few perfect tzadikim, one
should not rely [on R. Shimon b. Yochai's rule] saying: "I will not
work, rather my work will be performed by others, because I am a
perfect tzaddik." He may be mistaken, and not be a perfect tzaddik. This is what Abaye had in mind when he said: Many followed
R. Yishmael's advice [combining Torah learning with a worldly occupation,] and it worked well, for most people are not perfect tzaddikim like R. Shimon b. Yochai. This is supported by the Mishnah,
"Torah study is good together with an occupation". The Mishnah
continues: "All Torah study that is not joined with work will come
to naught in the end (Avos 2:2)."

However, in the Time to Come, when everyone will be righteous as it says, *Your people will all be righteous; they will inherit the*
land forever (Yeshayah 60:21), we will see the fulfillment of the
prophecy, *Foreigners will stand and tend your flocks and the sons of*
the stranger will be your plowmen and your vineyard workers
(Yeshayah 61:5).

HE GIVES WISDOM TO THE WISE

───═◉═───

BRACHOS 40a

GEMARA: Notice how the character of *Hakadosh Baruch Hu,* differs from that of mortal man. Mortal man can put something into an empty vessel but not into a full one. This is not so for Hakadosh Baruch Hu, who puts into a full vessel, [giving wisdom to the wise] but not into an empty one, as it says, *If you listened you will listen* (Shemos 15:26) . . . implying: If you listened to the old, you will be able to listen to the new.

The analogy fittingly compares the ear to a vessel. Speaking of idle talk, *Koheles* says, *All words are wearisome . . . the ear can hear only until it is full* (Koheles 1:8). The ear can only listen [to idle talk] until it has heard its fill. Idle talk is temporal, and therefore finite, with limited space. This is the character of Man; he can place things into an empty vessel, but he cannot put more things into it when the vessel is full.

However, G-d is not limited by space, for the whole world is filled with His glory. He is the place of the world, and He is not confined by the space of the world. Therefore, space filled with spirituality is limitless, able to hold infinite spirituality. Thus, when someone's mind is filled with abstract ideas, he can absorb a boundless flow of new ideas and thoughts. *If listening you will listen* means: If you listen to Torah thoughts you will continue to listen, learning more and more. However, a mind devoid of spiritual content cannot comprehend any spiritual concepts. If you do not [learn Torah], rather you fill your mind with things that have no spiritual content, you will not be able to grasp any abstract ideas.

G-D DESPISES HAUGHTINESS

——— ((●)) ———

BRACHOS 43b

GEMARA: If one walks four cubits with a stiffly erect posture it is as if he pushed the feet of the *Shechinah*.

Man is a chariot of the *Shechinah,* which hovers over his head, therefore, when he walks with a stiffly erect posture he pushes the feet of the *Shechinah.*

On the other hand, it says about one who conducts himself with humility and meekness, *I am with the despondent and the lowly of spirit* (Yeshayah 57:15). [A humble person] brings the *Shechinah* down to earth, as it says, *The whole world is filled with His glory* (Yeshayah 6:3).

THE CUP FOR *BIRKAS HAMAZON*

——— ((●)) ———

BRACHOS 51a

GEMARA: Ten things were said in connection with the cup used for *Birkas Hamazon.*

These ten things were said for *kedushah*—sanctity, and *taharah*—purity.

1. [The cup] needs to be rinsed inside and outside, to be clean and pure inside and out.

2. [The wine] must be *chai*—alive, [meaning, fresh and undiluted]⁸, because the *berachah* instills true *chaim* (life).

3. [The cup] should be full—so nothing should be missing in one's life.

4. It requires crowning, meaning one's disciples should sit around him—for the crown is His.

5. One should wrap himself. R. Papa wrapped himself in his robe, and R. Assi put on his turban [to say *Birkas Hamazon*]. For it says, *Prepare to meet your G-d, O Yisrael* (Amos 4:12). A turban [or hat] is worn so the fear of Heaven should be upon the one who says *Birkas Hamazon*.

6. It [the cup] must be raised with both hands—because the right side represents [the Divine attribute of] Mercy, and the left side symbolizes [the attribute of] Justice. [Raising the cup with both hands] is alluded to in the verse, *Lift your hands in the Sanctuary and bless Hashem* (Tehillim 134:2).

7. It must be placed in the right hand, so the Divine attribute of Mercy outweighs the attribute of Justice.

8. It must be raised a handbreadth—because it says, *I will lift up the cup of salvations, and the name of Hashem I will invoke* (Tehillim 116:13). [Why is it called *the cup of salvations*?] Because there are several places in Tanach that speak of the "cup of distress," such as, *To you [Edom], too, will the cup [of distress] pass. You will become drunk and you will vomit* (Eichah 4:21); *You have drunk from . . . the cup of bewilderment* (Yeshayah 51:17). The numeric value of cup—*kos* equals 86, which is the same numeric value as *Elo-him*, which represents the Divine attribute of Justice. Therefore [when lifting the cup for *Birkas Hamazon*] one stresses that *this* cup, which I bless with Hashem's name, is the *cup of salvations*—not one of affliction—for we do not say a *berachah* with Hashem's name over a cup of affliction. Rather he says, this cup I lift up in the name of Hashem, which denotes divine Mercy, turning the attribute of Justice into the attribute of Mercy.

---

8   In Talmudic times the wine was very strong and would only reach its potential after being diluted with water.

The Gemara in *Pesachim* 119b says that [in time to come when Yisrael will be vindicated] G-d will make a great banquet for the righteous, and David will be asked to lead the *Birkas Hamazon*. He will answer: *I will lift up the cup of salvations, and the name of Hashem I will invoke.*

9. One should fix his eyes on it—concentrating on the ideas we mentioned without distraction.

10. He passes it around to the members of his family—as a gift, for he who gives generously will be blessed.

FOUR MUST OFFER THANKS

BRACHOS 54b

GEMARA: There are four classes of people who must give thanks: Those crossing the sea, those traversing the desert, one who has recovered from an illness, and one who was released from jail. What is the source for those who crossed the sea? It says: *Those that go down to the sea in ships . . . Let them give thanks to Hashem for His kindness* (Tehillim 107:23-31). What is the source for those who traversed the desert? It says: *They wandered in the wilderness in a desert way . . . Let them give thanks to Hashem* (ibid. 4-8). What is the source for one who recovered from an illness? It says, *. . . Afflicted because of their iniquities . . . Let them give thanks to Hashem* (ibid. 17-21). What is the source for one who was set free from jail? It says, *Such as sat in darkness . . . are required to give thanks to Hashem* (ibid. 10-15).

A question may be asked: Psalm 107 opens with the phrase, *Give thanks to Hashem . . . those whom He redeemed from the hand of the enemy,* yet when listing the classes of people who must offer thanksgiving, the Gemara includes, those who traversed the desert, recovered from a sickness, and crossed the sea. These people were not redeemed from the hand of an enemy, rather they were redeemed from distress. Many other questions may be asked as well.

There are four obstacles, which prevent a person from attaining perfection and reaching his spiritual goal:

1. He has no income and must work hard to earn a livelihood [leaving no time for Torah study];

2. He is pursued by enemies, and therefore cannot serve Hashem the right way;

3. He has a sickly and frail constitution, which stands in the way of his Torah study and observance of mitzvos;

4. He has great wealth, and anxiety [about preserving it] keeps him from learning Torah and doing mitzvos.

These four obstacles and afflictions plague Yisrael in *galus,* as set forth in the chapter of Admonition (Devarim 28:15-69). The Midrash says that Yisrael's redemption from Egypt and deliverance from these four obstacles are indicated by the four times the word *cup* occurs in the dream of Pharaoh's chief butler (Bereishis 40:11-13). In keeping with this, we drink four cups at the *seder,* commemorating the redemption from Egypt.

This is also the underlying theme of the "four expressions of redemption", [*I will take you out; I will rescue you; I will liberate you;* and, *I will take you to Myself* (Shemos 6:6,7], because they were redeemed from these four adversities which are caused by the *galus.*

Correspondingly, Hashem will pour "four cups of bewilderment" on the idolaters, while giving Yisrael to drink "four cups of salvation," delivering them from the four sources of distress and scorn which are the scourges of *galus.*

Thus we are taught: "There are four classes of people who must offer thanks," for these four adversities prevent one from attaining

perfection. [At the redemption from Egypt] the Jews were saved
from all these adversities.

Psalm 107 begins with the words: *Give thanks to Hashem for He
is good* (107:1). This verse is expounded in the Gemara: It says, *As
they go out before the army, they say, "Give thanks to Hashem, for His
kindness endures forever"* (2 Divrei Hayamim 20:21), omitting the
phrase, *"for He is good,"* because the Holy One, blessed is He, does
not rejoice at the downfall of the wicked (Megillah 10b).[9] However, at the ultimate redemption, Yisrael will say, *for He is good*—
not because of the downfall of the wicked, but [as the psalm con-
tinues] because *they were redeemed by Hashem . . . from the hand of
distress* and from the four forms of adversity that tormented them.

The psalm continues, *whom He gathered from the lands, from
east and from west, from north and from the sea* (107:3), that is to
say, from the four exiles by the "four kingdoms." *From the east*, alludes to the kingdom of Media (Persia) which is east of Eretz
Yisrael; *From the north*, alludes to the kingdom of Babylonia which
is north of Eretz Yisrael; *from the west and from the sea*, alludes to
the kingdoms of Greece and Edom (Rome) which are to the west
of Eretz Yisrael. The verse mentions the west and the sea [which is
also west of Eretz Yisrael] but does not mention the south, because
none of the [four] kingdoms are in the south of Eretz Yisrael.

The psalm begins by mentioning the redemption from Egypt,
because it was the first liberation, and Egypt is south of Eretz
Yisrael. At that time they also were saved from the four obstacles
that stand in the way of attaining perfection, thus becoming worthy of receiving the Torah.

One Who Crossed the Desert

The Psalm says, *They wandered in the wilderness, in the desolation of
the path, they found no inhabited city* (107:4), this refers to the redemption from Egypt for they had difficulty with sustenance and

---

9   G-d's will is that the wicked repent, not, that they be destroyed. Therefore, the
phrase *for He is good* which connotes fulfillment of G-d's will is inappropriate in the
context of the destruction of the wicked (*Maharsha* to *Sanhedrin* 39b)

they skirted many countries until they arrived in a settled city in Eretz Yisrael.

Hungry as well as thirsty, their soul grew faint within them (107:5), refers to their time in the desert, as the Gemara says: [Our forefathers put Hashem to the test:] Twice because of water, twice because of the manna, and twice because of the quails (Arachin 15a). *They cried out to Hashem in their distress, He would rescue them from their straits* (107:6). He gave them the manna, the quails and the well [of Miriam].

He led them on a straight path, to go to an inhabited city (107:7), refers to their entrance to Eretz Yisrael. And for this, *Let them give thanks to Hashem for His kindness* (107:6), for in light of their sins in the wilderness, Hashem was not obligated to save them. He did it out of His kindness. For this reason the Sages enacted that after traversing a desert one should say [*birkas Hagomeil*, thanking G-d]: "Who bestows good things upon the guilty, who has bestowed every goodness on me."

The verse ends, *and His wonders to the children of man,* these are only considered wonders to the children of man who cannot enumerate all the praises of G-d, however to the Holy One, blessed be He, it is a small matter.

For He sated the yearning soul (107:9)—He supplied them with an abundance of good things in Eretz Yisrael, as it says, *[You will have] houses full of good things that you did not put there* (Devarim 6:11). Corresponding to this we drink the first Cup [at the *seder*].

One Freed From Prison

The next verse states, *Those who sat in darkness and the shadow of death* (107:10)—this alludes to the oppression by their enemies. In Egypt they were enslaved, living in the "darkness" of forced labor and in "the shadow of death" when their children were cast into the Nile.

The verse continues, *shackled in affliction and iron*—also alluding to their treatment in Egypt—as it says during the Exodus, *He brought you out of the iron crucible that was Egypt* (107:10).

The psalm continues, *They rebelled against the word of G-d*
(107:11)—because there were many sinners among them, and they
made the [idolatrous] "carved image of Michah."[10]

So He humbled their heart with hard labor (107:12)—this refers
to the slave labor they were forced to perform, and because of that,
they stumbled and there was none to help (107:12)—for even their
redeemer Moshe had run from Pharaoh.

Then they cried out to Hashem in their distress (107:13)—as it
says, *When they cried out because of their slavery, their pleas went up
before Hashem* (Shemos 2:23).

[For this,] *Let them give thanks to Hashem for His kindness*
(107:17).

For He smashed copper gates (107:17)—and led the Jews to freedom. This was a great miracle, for [until the Exodus] no slave ever
escaped from Egypt. [Therefore, a prisoner who was set free must
say *birkas Hagomeil,* and we commemorate this] by drinking the
second cup [at the Seder].

One Who Recovered From an Illness

The psalm continues, *Fools, because of their sinful path and because of
their iniquities, were afflicted* (107:17)—alluding to the sickness they
suffered in Egypt, as Hashem promised, *I will not strike you with any
of the sicknesses that I brought [on you] in Egypt. I am Hashem who
heals you* (Shemos 15:26). Sickness comes because of iniquity, as the
Gemara [defining the difference between transgressions and iniquities explains:] "Transgressions are rebellious acts which are not
cleansed by suffering; only death cleanses rebellious acts. Iniquities
are willful sins, and willful sins are cleansed by suffering (Yoma
36b)." This is implied by the above verse: *Fools, because of their sinful path and because of their iniquities, were afflicted*—If foolishness
pulled one to the path of transgressors, this is not a rebellious act;
rather it is an iniquity which is cleansed by suffering.

---

10   *Shofetim* ch.17.

Their soul abhorred all food (107:18)—Although his sickness caused his soul to abhor all food, and he could not eat, nevertheless, it is considered a fast and a suffering, which cleanses all willful iniquities.

They reached until the portals of death (107:18)—The Gemara in *Eruvin* 19a says: The wicked do not repent even at the gate of Gehinnom, but when this man reaches the gate of death and the portal of Gehinnom he is remorseful.

Then they cried out to Hashem in their distress, (107:19)—As the Gemara says: Crying out [to Hashem] is helpful even after one's verdict was announced and he has reached the gates of death (Rosh Hashanah 16a).

He would dispatch His word and cure them (107:20)—A human healer prescribes bandages, medications, and various treatments, but Hashem heals with just a simple word.

Let them give thanks to Hashem for His kindness (107:21)—as above.

And let them slaughter thanksgiving offerings and relate His works with joyful song (107:22)—If one's iniquities were not atoned through suffering, he would have to bring a guilt offering or a sin offering. But since he attained atonement through suffering and sickness, he need only bring a thanksgiving offering. From here we learn that all who have been saved from distress bring a thanksgiving offering. This is symbolized by the third cup [we drink at the Seder].

One Who Crossed the Sea

Psalm 107 continues: *Those who go down to the sea in ships* (107:23)—This refers to the anxiety that grips people who chase wealth, like those that go down to the sea in ships, as the Gemara in Eruvin 55a says: *[The Torah] is not across the sea* (Devarim 30:12)—[meaning, the Torah] is not found among merchants or dealers [who engage in maritime trade].

They [who go down in ships] have seen the deeds of Hashem, and His wonders in the watery deep (107:24). Just as *B'nei Yisrael* witnessed this at the Parting of the Sea, so do those that go down to the sea in ships see the deeds of Hashem, for [they see] the heavenly legions, as it says, *When I behold Your heavens, the work of Your fingers, the moon and the stars that You have set in place* (Tehillim 8:4), and *His wonders in the watery deep* (107:24), beneath the surface of the earth.

He spoke and raised the stormy wind and made the waves surge. They rose heavenward (107:25,26). The Gemara in *Bava Basra* 73a relates: [Rabbah said: Sailors told me:] "The height of a wave is three hundred *parsas*." [The sailors explained:] "One voyage, a wave lifted us so high, we saw the perch of the smallest star." Afterwards, *they plunged to the depths* (107:26). Having seen this, [the sailors] thought they understood [the mysteries of] what is above and what is beneath [the universe], but, *they reeled and staggered like a drunkard, and all their wisdom was swallowed up* (107:26), for it is impossible to know [the mysteries of] what is above and what is beneath [the universe,] as it says in *Chagigah* 11b,16a. *Then they cried out to Hashem in their distress, and He saved them from their troubles* (107:28).

In light of this, the Gemara concludes: Most sailors are God-fearing (Kiddushin 82a).

The storm restored calmness, the waves were stilled (107:29). The storm itself, which made the waves surge restored calmness, so that *the waves were stilled*. As the Gemara in *Sanhedrin* 91a says: The instrument with which He crushes, He uses to heal. [The storm raged, and the storm calmed the waves.]

Let them give thanks to Hashem for His kindness, and His wonders to the children of man (107:31). [Those who crossed the sea should recite the berachah *Hagomeil*]. Accordingly, we drink the fourth cup [at the *Seder*].

The Order of the Four Categories

Psalm 107 lists the four categories of people who should give thanks, in the following order: (1) traversing a desert, (2) being released from prison, (3) being healed from sickness, (4) crossing the sea. However, the Gemara enumerates them in a different order: (1) crossing the sea, (2) traversing the desert, (3) being healed from sickness, (4) being released from prison.

Furthermore, in the case of "sea" and "desert" the Gemara uses the present tense: "those crossing the sea", "those traversing the desert," whereas in the case of "sickness" and "prison" the Gemara uses the past tense: "one who was sick and was healed," and, "one who was freed from prison."

[Why does the order of the Gemara differ from that of the psalm?] The order of the Gemara corresponds to the underlying idea of the Four Cups, [which commemorates miracles of the Exodus in their historical order].

At the Exodus, *B'nei Yisrael* were liberated from the four obstacles [that hampered their devotion to Hashem]. The first category in the Gemara is "those crossing the sea," for when B'nei Yisrael crossed the sea, they gained the enormous wealth of the "spoils of Egypt" [that washed up from the sea]. For this they thanked Hashem by singing the *Shiras Hayam* (the Song of the Sea). As a remembrance of this the Sages instituted the first Cup of the *Kiddush* [at the *seder*] in which we say "a memorial of the Exodus from Egypt," affirming that G-d created the world.

The Gemara's second category is, "those crossing the desert," for in the desert they suffered many afflictions until they were granted the gifts of the quail and the manna. As a remembrance of this the Sages instituted the Second Cup [at the *seder*] before the meal, [when we are still hungry] as an expression of thanks to Hashem through the Song of the Well (Bamidbar 21:18-20).

The third category is "one who was healed from sickness," because at the Giving of the Torah all the sick were healed from the diseases they had contracted in Egypt. As a remembrance of this the Sages instituted the Third Cup of the *seder*, after we have eaten the meal, unlike a sick person who can neither eat nor drink.

The Gemara's fourth category is that of "a prisoner who was set free," because *B'nei Yisrael* did not gain complete freedom until they conquered Eretz Yisrael, and domination by our enemies ended. As a remembrance of this the Fourth Cup was instituted.

INTERPRETATION OF DREAMS

BRACHOS 55b

GEMARA: All dreams follow the mouth [of the interpreter; they are fulfilled according to his interpretation].

The *Baal Ha'akeidah* discusses this topic at great length, explaining how the meaning of a dream can change according to the good or ill wishes of the interpreter. But his explanations do not solve the difficulties.

It seems to me, the subject should be understood according to its simple, literal meaning. Some dreams have a variety of interpretations—some good, some bad. About such dreams Rava said: [An interpretation comes true only] if it corresponds to the content of the dream. And if such a dream is not interpreted, it is of no consequence. Rav Chisda said about such dreams: A dream that is not interpreted is like a letter that was not read. Rashi explains: Since neither good nor bad was read into it [it has no effect], for all such dreams follow their interpretation.

[Dreams with obvious intent will come true even without interpretation.] However, even an obviously favorable dream can be reversed by an unfavorable interpretation, as may be seen from the saying: If one sees a well in his dream he should rise early and say: *A well of living waters* (Shir Hashirim 4:15), before an ominous verse comes to mind, such as, *As a well flows with waters, so she flows with wickedness* (Yirmeyah 6:7).

This is not odd, because man has the power to make good things happen by taking a favorable view, as it says, *One with a good eye will bless* (Mishlei 22:9). Conversely, a person can make bad things happen through his [evil] eye, as Bilam did. Furthermore, one can make good or bad things happen simply by uttering words, as it says: The blessing given by an ordinary person should not be unimportant in your eyes (Berachos 7a); nor should a curse given by an ordinary person be unimportant in your eyes (Megillah 15a). Here too, the mouth was given the power to make a dream come true according to the words one utters, provided it corresponds to the content of the dream.

Summary

According to the Gemara we can differentiate between three kinds of dreams:

1. A dream that is fulfilled only according to the words of the interpreter. Without an interpretation this dream [is meaningless;] portending neither good nor evil. About such a dream Rav Chisda said: A dream that is not interpreted is like a letter that was not read; [it has no effect]. The dream of Rabbi Bana'ah[11] with its twenty-four interpretations, and the various dreams that were interpreted by Bar Hedya[12], were of this type. Such dreams are initiated by demons. Without an interpretation these dreams are meaningless.

2. A dream that has an obvious meaning. It will be fulfilled even if it is not interpreted, but it can be reversed by an interpretation, from good to bad or from bad to good, as in the case of one who sees a well in his dream, as was mentioned above. Of this type was also the dreams of Pharaoh's two officials [the butler and the baker,] who dreamed of future events, as Rabbi Yehoshua says in connection with the verse, *On the grapevine there were three tendril* (Bereishis 40:10). This kind of dream is stimulated by the heavenly constellations.

---

[11] R. Bana'ah said: "I had a dream, and went to twenty-four interpreters, each gave a different interpretation, and all of them came true." (Berachos 55b)

[12] Bar Hedya was an interpreter of dreams, who gave favorable interpretations to one who paid, and unfavorable interpretations to one who did not pay. (Berachos 56a)

3. A dream with only one true meaning, which cannot be changed or reversed [through an interpretation]. Yosef's dreams are in this category. Such dreams are inspired by an angel, as it says, [*Hashem said about Moshe:*] *In a dream will I speak with him* (Bamidbar 12:6).

People fast when they have an ominous dream because perhaps it was brought on by an angel, and if so it cannot be changed through a favorable interpretation. It can only be given an auspicious outcome through *teshuvah* and good deeds.

THE TORAH CONTAINS THE TOTALITY
OF ALL KNOWLEDGE

BRACHOS 58a

GEMARA: If one sees a great gathering of Jews, he should say: Blessed is the Knower of Secrets [meaning, He knows the secrets in each person's heart (Rashi)]. . . . We learn in a Braisa that a great gathering is not less than 600,000 Jews.

Since a "great gathering" means 600,000 people, there are 600,000 different views, which include all opinions, in this group. For this reason the Torah was given to 600,000 Jews in the wilderness, because the Torah includes the totality of all views and wisdom. [Because the Torah was given to the entire range of opinions,] nothing can be added to it.

Any new idea a future sage will discover was already given at Sinai, in the mind of one of the 600,000 people who were standing at Sinai.

THE *BERACHAH* WHEN SEEING
A TORAH SCHOLAR

BRACHOS 58a

GEMARA: Upon seeing an outstanding Torah scholar one should say: Blessed is He, Who has apportioned of His knowledge to those who fear Him. Upon seeing an outstanding scholar of other nations one should say: Blessed is He, Who has given of His knowledge to human beings.

When seeing a Torah scholar one says, "Who has apportioned of His knowledge," because Torah scholars are His portion, His inheritance and His share. It is as if He shares His knowledge, which is the Torah, with them. [Torah scholars] are called "those who fear Him," because they acquire knowledge through fear of sin, as it says: Anyone whose fear of sin takes priority over his wisdom, his wisdom will endure (Avos 3:11).

But G-d does not share the wisdom of His Torah with scholars of other nations. Rather, He grants them general wisdom.

Similarly, when honoring Jewish kings one should say [the *berachah*]: "Who apportioned of His glory to those who fear Him," for [their glory comes from the true glory] of the Torah. However, He only grants worldly glory to gentile rulers.

THE SEVEN *SEFIROS*

BRACHOS 58a

GEMARA: [R. Shila expounded the verse:] *Yours, Hashem is the greatness, the strength, the splendor, the*

*triumph, and the glory. Even everything in heaven
and earth. Yours, Hashem is the kingdom, and the sovereignty over every leader* (1 Divrei Hayamim 29:11).

Yours, Hashem is the greatness, refers to the
work of Creation. *The strength,* refers to the
Exodus from Egypt. *The splendor,* refers to the
sun and the moon which stood still for Yehoshua
(Yehoshua 10:13). *And the triumph,* refers to the
fall of Rome. *And the glory,* refers to the battle of
the valleys of Arnon (Bamidbar 21:14). *Even
everything in heaven and earth,* refers to the battle
of Sisra. *Yours, Hashem is the kingdom,* refers to
the war against Amalek. *And the sovereignty,* refers
to the war of Gog and Magog.[13]

T he events described in R. Shila's exposition are not listed in
historical order; the fall of Rome is listed before the battle of
the valleys of Arnon [which happened at the end of Yisrael's wan-
dering in the desert], and before the battle of Sisra. Similarly, R.
Akiva, in his exposition [of the same verse], lists the splitting of the
Sea before the slaying of the first-born.

The verse in *Divrei Hayamim* enumerates the seven Divine attributes in the order of the seven "lower" *sefiros* as they are
arranged by the Kabbalists.[14] R. Shilah explains the Divine attrib-

---

[13] *Yechezkel,* ch. 38 and 39 foretell the climactic war of Gog and Magog which will
usher in the End of Days and the era of Mashiach.

[14] The *sifrei Kabbalah* teach that the Divine Infinite Light descends from the
Throne of G-d to our physical universe through a series of ten *sefiros.* The *sefiros* are
commonly called "attributes," "vessels," "channels" or "emanations." It is impossible to grasp the reality of the *sefiros* for they are beyond human understanding.

The Infinite Light flows down through the three "uppermost" unfathomable *sefiros: Keser*—Crown, *Chochmah*—Wisdom, *Binah*—Understanding, continuing
through the seven "lower" *Sefiros: Gedulah*—Greatness [also called *Chesed*—
Kindness], *Gevurah*—Power, *Tiferes*—Beauty, *Netzach*—Triumph, *Hod*—Splendor,
Yesod—Foundation, ending in *Malchus.* This is the order which they are listed in the
verse in *Divrei Hayamim.*

utes as they are manifest through the *sefiros*, whereby Hashem acts according to the specific attribute of each of the seven *sefiros*.

And so R. Shilah expounds:

Yours, Hashem is the Gedulah—Greatness, for *Gedulah* is the *sefirah* of *Chesed*—Kindness, the *sefirah* by which the world was created, as it says, *The world is built on chesed*—kindness (Tehillim 89:3).

With the attribute of *Gevurah*—Power, Hashem brought about the Exodus through the plagues He inflicted on the Egyptians, as it says, *Yisrael saw the great hand that Hashem had wrought against Egypt* (Shemos 14:31). Although the word *great* generally refers to the attribute of Kindness, when it is combined with the word *hand* it alludes to *Gevurah*—Power, which is symbolized by a hand.

With the attribute of *Tiferes*—Beauty, or Eminence, Hashem caused the sun and the moon to stand still [in the days of Yehoshua] bringing renown and eminence to Yehoshua.

With the attribute of *Netzach*—Triumph, Hashem caused the downfall of Rome, as it says, *Their lifeblood spurted out [Vayaz] on My garments* (Yeshayah 63:3).

With the attribute of *Hod*—Splendor, Hashem performed the miracles in the valleys of Arnon, as it says *Therefore it will be told in the book of the miracles of Hashem that which He did at the Red sea, and at the valleys of Arnon.*

Even everything in heaven and earth—According to the Kabbalists this denotes the *Yesod*—Foundation. It alludes to the victory in the battle [in which Devorah defeated Sisera,] the Canaanite general, as it says, *From heaven they fought* (Shofetim 5:20).

The *Sefirah* of *Malchus*—Kingdom is expressed in the verse, *Yours, Hashem is the kingdom*—With the attribute of *Malchus*, Hashem brought about the defeat of Amalek. As it says, *For the hand is on the throne (keis) of G-d; Hashem maintains a war against Amalek, from generation to generation* (Shemos 17:16). The word *throne (keis)* suggests *Malchus*—Kingdom. [*K*eis should be written as *kisei*, however the *alef* is missing,] because G-d's throne (*kisei*) will not be complete [and the missing *alef* will not be restored] until the offspring of Amalek is destroyed.

And the sovereignty—In time to come, Hashem will exalt Himself with all these attributes. This will happen in the war of Gog and Magog, as it says [in the prophecy about this war], *I will be exalted and I will be sanctified and I will make Myself known before the eyes of many nations; then they will know that I am Hashem* (Yechezkel 38:23).

RABBI AKIVA'S INTERPRETATION

58a GEMARA: *Yours, Hashem is the greatness, the strength, the splendor, the triumph and the glory* (1 Divrei Hayamim 29:11).

R. Akiva expounded: *Yours, Hashem is the greatness*, refers to the splitting of the Sea. *The strength*, refers to the slaying of the first-born; *the splendor*, refers to the Giving of the Torah; *and the triumph*, this refers to Yerushalayim; *and the glory*, refers to the Beis Hamikdash.

Yours, Hashem is the greatness (*Gedulah*), refers to the splitting of the Sea, for through the Divine attribute of Kindness (*Chesed* or *Gedulah*) the Jews walked across the Sea and were saved.

The strength—refers to the slaying of the first-born. For at the slaying of the first-born the Egyptians were judged through the Divine attribute of Justice.

The glory—refers to the Giving of the Torah which brought renown and glory to Yisrael, as it says, *For [the Torah] is your wisdom and discernment in the eyes of the peoples* (Devarim 4:6).

The triumph—refers to Yerushalayim, for it represents the triumph of Yisrael, as it says, *Yerushalayim, mountains enfold it* (Tehillim 125:2).

The splendor—refers to the Beis Hamikdash, which is the splendor and glory of Yisrael.

FASHIONED WITH WISDOM

───≈◉≈───

BRACHOS 60b

> GEMARA: After coming out of the bathroom one
> should say the *berachah*: Blessed are You Hashem
> . . . Who fashioned man with wisdom and created
> within him many openings and many cavities.

A ccording to Rashi, the phrase, "Who fashioned man with
wisdom" refers to the clause that follows it, that G-d
formed man wisely, creating within him many openings . . .

According to *Tosafos*, the phrase, "Who has fashioned man with
wisdom" is an independent statement. Hashem used wisdom when
He created man, by preparing his food before creating him.

Alternatively, the phrase can be interpreted to mean that
Hashem endowed man with wisdom and discernment, unlike all
other living creatures, which were not granted wisdom.

NEFESH, RUACH, NESHAMAH

───≈◉≈───

BRACHOS 60b

> GEMARA: When one wakes up in the morning, he
> should say: "My G-d, the soul You placed within
> me is pure. You created it, You fashioned it, and
> You breathed it into me."

T he word *neshamah*—soul, when used in the Torah, includes
the three levels of the soul: *nefesh*—man's instinct of self-

preservation; *ruach*—the spirit that gives man the power to speak; *neshamah*—which gives man intellect, knowledge and understanding. This is the way the Kabbalists and the philosophers define *neshamah*.

In line with this, the *berachah* of *Elokai neshamah shenasata bi* uses three expressions:

"You created it [*berasah*]"—this refers to *nefesh*, the basic life force, about which it says, *G-d created* (vayivra) *man* (Bereishis 1:27).

"You formed it [*yetzartah*]"—this refers to *ruach*, the spirit of life, about which it says *Hashem formed [vayitzer] man* (Bereishis 2:7).

"You breathed it into me [*nefachtah bi*]"—this refers to the *neshamah* which endows man with intellect, as it says, *He breathed [vayipach] into his nostrils the soul of life* (Bereishis 2:7).

THE TORAH IS ESSENTIAL
FOR YISRAEL'S SURVIVAL

BRACHOS 61b

GEMARA: The [Roman] government issued a decree forbidding the Jews to study Torah. Papas ben Yehudah found Rabbi Akiva gathering people in public assemblies and teaching them Torah. He asked, Aren't you afraid of the government? Said Rabbi Akiva: Let me explain it to you with a parable: A fox was walking by the river bank, and saw swarms of fish moving from place to place. Said the fox to the fish: Why are you running? They replied: We are trying to avoid the nets that the

sons of Adam set to trap us. Said the fox: Why
don't you come up on dry land, then you and I
can live together in the way my ancestors lived
with your ancestors. They answered: If we are in
danger in the water, which is our natural habitat,
surely we will be in danger [on dry land], an en-
vironment in which we would die!

The explanation of the parable is as follows: The fox represents the idolaters who are compared to unclean wild beasts.
The fish symbolize the Jewish people, as the Gemara says: [R.
Yochanan said:] I am an offspring of Yosef over whom the evil eye
has no power (Berachos 20a) . . . . Just as the fishes in the sea are
covered by water and the evil eye has no power over them, so the
evil eye has no power over the offspring of Yosef. We have explained elsewhere that this refers not only to Yosef, but to all of
Yisrael.

The fish "running from place to place" refers to Rabbi Akiva
gathering them together in public assemblies to teach Torah.

The "nets that the sons of Adam set to trap us" stands for the
evil decrees the Romans forced upon us, for we interpret "sons of
Adam" as the *"sons of Edom"*, the Romans. The nations of the
world want us to come up on dry land and live together with them,
abandoning the Torah of Moshe which is represented by the water,
as it says, *Ho, everyone who is thirsty, go to the water* (Yeshayah 55:1).
Thus the Roman emperor said to R. Tanchum: "Come, let us live
together and become one nation the way my ancestors lived with
your ancestors." They want us to neglect Torah study, as we did at
the time of the destruction of the first *Beis Hamikdash*, which was
laid waste *because they forsook My Torah* (Yirmeyah 9:12).

We answer them, Just as the fish cannot leave the water, so too,
we cannot abandon the Torah.

HASHEM SHARES OUR DISTRESS

BRACHOS 63a

GEMARA: R. Huna said: Whoever makes the Name
of heaven a partner with his suffering will have his
sustenance doubled.

Rashi explains this to mean that [the one who suffers] bless-
es Hashem even for evil, [saying the *berachah* of *Dayan
Ha'emes*—Blessed are You Hashem . . . the true Judge.] But this
does not fit with the word partner!

We may explain this as follows: We know Hashem accompanies
one who is suffering, as Hashem says: *I am with him in distress*
(Tehillim 91:15). The person who is suffering should pray that
Hashem help him for His Name's sake, for He is suffering with us.
According to this interpretation, he is indeed making Hashem's
Name a partner with his suffering, as it says, *Shad-dai will be with
you in your distress* (Iyov 22:25).

MESECHTA SHABBOS

THE HOLINESS OF G-D'S NAME

SHABBOS 10b

GEMARA: A person may not greet his fellow saying, *Shalom!*—"Peace!"—in [an unseemly place such as] a bathhouse, [because *Shalom* is a name of G-d] as it says, *Gidon built an altar there, and He called it "Hashem-Shalom"* (Shofetim 6:24).

[Asks the Gemara:] If so, it should also be forbidden to say the word *emunah*—"faith" in a bathhouse, since it says, *HaKeil hane'eman*—*"He is the faithful G-d"* (Devarim 7:9). Yet, Rava b. Mechasia says: One is allowed to say the word *emunah*—faith—in a bathhouse! [The Gemara answers:] The word "faithful" is used as an adjective, rather than a proper name of G-d, however, *Shalom* is used as a name of G-d.

Since Hashem makes peace and is faithful, why is *Shalom*—Peace—in fact a Holy Name, while *Ne'eman*—faithful—is only an adjective?

Furthermore, there are many other descriptive terms for G-d, such as, *Rachum ve*Chanun—*Merciful and Gracious*—(Shemos 34:6), which don't have the sanctity of a proper Name of Hashem.

This may be answered based on the following *Midrash*: When Hashem wished to create man, a dispute arose in Heaven. Kindness said: "Man should be created, for he performs acts of kindness." Truth said: "He should not be created, for he tells nothing but lies." Righteousness said: "Man should be created, for he acts righteously." Peace said: "He should not be created, for he quarrels all the time." [Thus, man possesses the qualities of kindness and righteousness, but he lacks the traits of truth and peace.]

55

[According to the above Midrash,] the names of G-d which may
be erased and are not holy, such as Merciful, Gracious, Abundant
in Kindness, and Slow to Anger, denote qualities of G-d that are
also manifest in man. Since man is also compassionate and merciful, these attributes are only adjectives, not names of G-d, and may
be said in the bathhouse. However, *Shalom*, "Peace" is a quality
not found in man, therefore, *Shalom* is truly a name of G-d, for He
alone makes peace. Similarly, since *Emes* "Truth" is a quality not
found in man, the seal of G-d is called *Emes*.

Tosafos in *Sotah* says that G-d's name *Shalom*, which may not be
recited in a bathroom, may also not be erased. However, it not forbidden to erase the word *emes* nor say the word *emes* in a bathroom,
because although G-d's seal is called *emes*, because it is a quality not
shared with man, it is never used as an actual name of G-d.

WHO IS WEALTHY?

SHABBOS 25b

GEMARA: Rabbi Tarfon said: Who is wealthy? He
who possesses a hundred vineyards, a hundred fields,
and a hundred slaves working in them. Rav Akiva
says, one who has a wife whose actions are pleasing.
Rav Yosi says, one who has a toilet near his house.

T he sayings of these Rabbis can be explained as follows: Some
people amass wealth in order to gain honor and prestige,
making a name for themselves, and becoming known as a magnate.
Others seek wealth thinking they need a great deal of money to
supply their wives with exquisite delicacies, elegant clothing and
jewelry. Others pursue riches because they want to protect themselves against poverty in the event of sickness.

Rabbi Tarfon is talking to the rich man who amasses wealth because he craves glory and recognition, saying he will be rich when he owns a hundred vineyards, a hundred fields, and a hundred slaves working in them. The term one hundred is an exaggeration, implying that he who seeks wealth will never be content, for *A lover of money will never be satisfied with money* (Koheles 5:9). Rabbi Tarfon explains, that his craving for fame and recognition will never be fulfilled.

Addressing the person who accumulates riches to pay for luxuries and elegant clothes for his wife, Rabbi Akiva says he will never have enough wealth, for she will have an insatiable appetite for the pleasures to which she has become accustomed.

The truly rich man has a wife whose deeds are beautiful, and does not demand an abundance of jewelry and frills from her husband. [He is rich] because he is satisfied with very little, as the Mishnah puts it: Who is wealthy? He who is happy with his share.

Rabbi Akiva had his exemplary wife Rachel, in mind. Though she was the daughter of [the wealthy] Kalba Savua, Rachel was satisfied with very little. [When Kalba Savua heard that his daughter was betrothed to the poor and unlearned shepherd Akiva he disinherited her. In spite of their abject poverty, she encouraged Akiva to leave home, learn Torah and become a Torah scholar. After 24 years of learning Torah, Rabbi Akiva returned accompanied by 24,000 disciples.] When Rachel came out to greet him, her neighbors told her: ["You are not properly dressed to greet such a great scholar.] Borrow some respectable clothing." She replied, *The righteous one knows his animal's soul* (Mishlei 12:10), [meaning, Rabbi Akiva knows why I don't have dignified clothing.]

Addressing the man who hoards money thinking he will need it in time of sickness, Rabbi Yosi says: No amount of money will allay your anxiety. [Instead of pursuing money] make sure you stay in good health, as it says: Who is wealthy? He who has a toilet near his table.[15]

---

[15]   In his time, toilets were mostly out in the field, and sanitary conditions were very primitive. Having a toilet in the house would go a long way toward promoting good health.

TRYING TO INFURIATE HILLEL

SHABBOS 31a

GEMARA: [Hillel was known to be very calm and gentle.] A man wagered with his friend that he would cause Hillel to become angry. One Friday afternoon, as Hillel was preparing for Shabbos, the man interrupted him, asking: "Why are the heads of Babylonians cyclical?" Hillel replied calmly, "My son, you have asked a very important question. It is because they don't have intelligent midwives."

[He then asked:] "Why are the Tarmodeans weak-eyed?" [Hillel replied:] "Because they live in a sandy place, [and the wind constantly blows the sand into their eyes].

He then asked: Why are the feet of Africans wide?" [Hillel replied:] "Because they live in marshy places [and their wide feet keep them from sinking into the swamp.]

Although Hillel was tolerant, why did he answer secular questions, unrelated to Torah themes? Did not Shlomoh say: *Do not answer a fool according to his foolishness* (Mishlei 26:4)?

Possibly, the humble Hillel did not believe the man intended to provoke him; rather he thought the man was indeed asking questions pertaining to Torah themes, hinting at the three deplorable character traits of the disciples of Bilam—an arrogant spirit, an evil eye, and a greedy soul (Avos 5:22).

In the first question Hillel addressed the evil trait of arrogance. He understood the question, "Why are the heads of the Babylonians cyclical?" to mean, "Why have the Babylonians lost their fortune?" For the Gemara says: Wealth and poverty are a continuous cycle in the world.

Hillel answered: "Because they don't have intelligent midwives," meaning, the Babylonians are arrogant, a trait only found in one who is foolish and devoid of intelligence. Arrogance and foolishness are typical Babylonian traits, as it says: "Hypocrisy and arrogance are rampant in Babylonia (Sanhedrin 24a)." [Their arrogance], stemming from their lack of intelligence caused the "cyclical form of their heads," or, the turnabout of their fortune, from wealth to poverty.

A Second Attempt

When the man asked, "Why are the Tarmodeans weak-eyed?", Hillel thought he was referring to the second bad trait mentioned in *Avos*, namely, "An evil eye." For the Gemara says, the people of the generation of the Flood became arrogant [and sinned] because of the [freedom they exercised with] the eyeball (Sanhedrin 108a). Rashi explains: By gazing upon their own perfect prosperity, they became haughty, and lusted after whatever they saw. In many places, immorality, is symbolized by the eye, as the Gemara says: Shimshon [rebelled] against G-d through his eyes, therefore the Philistines put out his eyes (Sotah 9a). Similarly, the Tarmodians were guilty of immorality, which caused the weakness in their eyes.

Hillel answered: Because they live in sandy places. [The Hebrew word for sand is *Chol*, which also translates as "profane." In other words they are vulgar people], who have no *kedushah*, to restrain them from immorality.

A Third Attempt

When the man asked, "Why are the feet of Africans wide?", Hillel thought the questioner was referring to the third bad character trait mentioned in *Avos*, namely, "a greedy soul," [for feet are symbolic of wealth,] as it says: "A man's wealth puts him on his feet" (Pesachim 119a).

Hillel answered: Because they live in *bitz'ei mayim*—marshy places. The word [*betza*, means both "swamp" and "money"] implying that Africans live among idol worshippers who love *betza* (money). The people of Africa are descendants of Canaan who left Eretz Yisrael. The Gemara says that Canaan commanded his sons to love robbery and money (Sanhedrin 91a).

REUVEN'S ERROR

SHABBOS 55b

GEMARA: [The Torah relates that Reuven lived with Bilhah, his father's concubine (Bereishis 35:22). Addressing this incident,] Rav Shmuel bar Nachman said: Whoever says Reuven sinned is mistaken, for it says [in the same verse], *Yaakov had twelve sons*, which teaches us that all of Yaakov's sons were equal [in righteousness.]

Rashi explains: [Since Reuven interfered with Yaakov's sleeping arrangements,[16] the Torah considers it as if he had committed adultery with Bilhah].

The Torah uses the metaphor "living with Bilhah", for moving his father's bed, because Rachel was the mainstay of the household. In fact, Yaakov worked [for Lavan for fourteen years] for the right to marry Rachel, and it was for Rachel's sake that he married Leah

---

[16] After Rachel's death, Yaakov moved his bed to the tent of Bilhah, Rachel's handmaid. Reuven saw this as an insult to his mother Leah, and took it upon himself to move Yaakov's bed to Leah's tent.

and the two handmaids [Bilhah and Zilpah]. Therefore, as long as Rachel was alive Yaakov's bed was always in Rachel's tent. After her death, he moved his bed into the tent of her loyal maidservant Bilhah, in her honor.

The Gemara in *Yevamos* says that Avraham and his descendants were forbidden to marry non-Jewish maidservants. Avraham was allowed to marry Hagar because since he owned her, [by marrying her,] she became free. This is based on the *halachah* that if a master marries off his slave to a free woman, the slave is thereby set free. So too, when Yaakov married the two handmaids Bilhah and Zilpah, they became free women.

Reuven mistakenly believed that Bilhah and Zilpah did not become free [by marriage to Yaakov]. Therefore, Reuven called the sons of Bilhah and Zilpah slaves, for the son of a handmaid is indeed a slave.

Because Reuven thought Bilhah was a slave, he resented [the fact that Yaakov placed his bed in Bilhah's tent,] considering it an insult to his mother. [Indignantly] he said: "If my mother's sister Rachel was my mother's rival, should the handmaid of my mother's sister now be my mother's rival?"

Following Reuven's [mistaken] train of thought, one could reason that being a maidservant, Bilhah was not legally married to Reuven's father and as such would not be prohibited to Reuven. Since Reuven thought he was permitted to cohabit with Bilhah, the Torah regards it as though he actually lived with her. That is why it says, *He was the firstborn, but when he defiled his father's bed his birthright was given to the sons of Yosef* (1 Divrei Hayamim 5:1).

The Gemara explains: By moving [his father's bed] from Bilhah's tent, Reuven offended the honor of Rachel, the mainstay of the household. Therefore the birthright was taken from him and given to Yosef, Rachel's firstborn.

HEALING OF SPIRIT AND BODY

SHABBOS 67a

GEMARA: R. Yochanan said: One who has an inflammatory fever should tie a white twisted thread
around a rose bush, and make a slight notch in it
with an iron knife. On the first day [of the sick-
ness] he should say: *And the angel of G-d appeared
to him in the flame out of the midst of the bush. He
saw: And behold the bush is burning with fire, and
the bush is not consumed!* (Shemos 3:2). On the
second day he should make another slight notch
saying: *Moshe said: Now let me turn aside that I
may see this great sight—why does the bush not burn
up* (3:3). On the third day, again making a small
notch, he should say: *When Hashem saw that he
had turned aside to see, G-d called out to him from
the midst of the bush* (3:4).

L et us explain why reciting these three verses will bring healing for inflammatory fever.

The Rambam in *Shemonah Perakim* ("Eight Chapters") says that
diseases of the body correspond to diseases of the soul, as the
Gemara expounds the verse, *Place* [vesamtem] *these words [of Torah]
of Mine on your heart and your soul* (Devarim 11:18)—the word *ve-
samtem* should be read as *sam-tam*, "a perfect remedy", [meaning
the Torah is a remedy for body and soul] (Kiddushin 30b).

This may be compared to a man who hit his son, wounding him
badly. He then bandaged the wound, saying: "Son! As long as this
bandage is on your wound, you may eat and drink whatever you
please and bathe in hot or cold water without fear, but without the
bandage, your wound will fester." So, too, the Holy One, blessed

be He, said to Yisrael: "My children! I created the *yetzer hara* (the evil impulse), symbolized by the wound, but I also created the Torah as its antidote. If you learn Torah, you will not fall into the clutches of the *yetzer hara*; if not, you will be delivered into his hand."

Sickness of the body is tied to sickness of the soul. This is evident from the verse, *If you obey Hashem your G-d, and do what is upright in His eyes,* by observing the Torah, which brings healing for the soul, *then I will not strike you with the sicknesses that I brought on Egypt. I am Hashem who heals you;* (Shemos 15:26).

This does not contradict the Gemara, which says it is forbidden to learn Torah to remedy sickness (Shavuos 15b), because the Gemara permits learning Torah to ward off sickness.

However another Gemara appears contradictory: "If someone has a headache, let him engage in Torah study. If he feels pain over his entire body, let him engage in Torah study, for it says, *It is a healing for his whole body* (Mishlei 1:9)" (Eruvin 54a). This Gemara seems to indicate that one may learn Torah as a remedy, yet previously we said it is forbidden to study Torah as a cure for sickness!

According to the principle [that sicknesses of the body and spirit are interrelated] a person may learn Torah as a remedy for his spiritual ailment, and his physical sickness will also be cured. The Sages prohibited the healing of physical ailments by uttering incantations if there is no intention to heal the spirit. However if one learns Torah for the sake of spiritual healing, his physical ailments will be cured at the same time.

The Gemara says: "If someone has a headache let him engage in Torah study." Why doesn't it say: Let him engage in "the words of Torah," as in the berachah: "Who has commanded us to engross ourselves 'in the words of Torah'"?

The Gemara says: "Speech is harmful for one suffering from headaches or eye sickness" (Nedarim 41a). Since speech is harmful to one with a headache, he cannot engage in "words of Torah"; however he should mentally engage in Torah study, or support Torah institutions [which does not involve speech]. This learning will heal his spirit, bringing cure to his physical headache as well.

With this we can explain why reciting the three verses [of Moshe's vision of the burning bush] can remedy inflammatory fever.

The vision of the burning bush alluded to the plagues to be brought on Egypt. The Jews at that time, having adopted the abominable idolatrous life-style of Egypt, were spiritually sick, unworthy of being saved from the torment that was to befall the Egyptians. Moshe's question *Why doesn't the bush burn up?*, meant, "In what merit will they be saved from the sickness and the plagues of Egypt?" Hashem answered, *"I am the G-d of your fathers, the G-d of Avraham, the G-d of Yitzchak, and the G-d of Yaakov . . . ,"* meaning, "[They will be saved] in the merit of the Fathers and the Torah they will receive."

Since the three verses (Shemos 3:2,3,4) speak about healing of the spirit, they are also recited for inflammatory fever on three successive days as a remedy for the body. The *Shechinah* appears to a patient with three days of burning fever, as it says, *Hashem will fortify him on the bed of misery* (Tehillim 41:4). Concerning this situation we can also ask, "Why does the bush not burn"? [In what merit will he be saved]? for the Gemara says: "The miracle done for a sick person is greater than the miracle performed for Chananiah, Mishael, and Azariah, [who were saved from the fiery furnace]; the miracle of Chananiah, Mishael, and Azariah concerned a man-made fire, which can be extinguished by man, whereas the fire [fever] of a sick person is a heavenly fire, which cannot be extinguished" (Nedarim 41a). . .

THE WEAK WILL OVERPOWER THE MIGHTY

SHABBOS 77b

GEMARA: Rav Yehudah says: The Holy One, blessed be He, did not create anything in His world without purpose. The snail is a remedy for a scab. The fly is a cure for a hornet's sting, [for crushed flies placed on a hornet's sting, will bring relief (Rashi)]. [Crushed] mosquitos are a remedy for snakebite. Snakes were created as a remedy for boils. A [crushed] spider is an antidote for a scorpion's bite.

Rav Yehudah does not mean to list the purpose of each and every creature, for if so, one may ask: Why were the hornet, the boil, and the scorpion themselves created?

Rav Yehudah mentions snails, flies, and mosquitos because they are tiny creatures which people might think there is no need for them. Therefore, he explains that even these insignificant creatures fulfill an important function as antidotes against the poisonous sting [of hornets, snakes, and scorpions.]

It was not necessary to explain why hornets, boils, snakes and scorpions were created. These were obviously created to admonish and punish [wrongdoers]. Thus the Gemara continues: "There are five cases where the weak strike fear into the strong: a mosquito arouses fear in an elephant; a *mafgia*[17] strikes fear in a lion . . ," teaching us that a person should not rely on his power and might [to commit injustice], for Hashem has many messengers [to exact retribution]. Do not think tiny creatures like snails, flies, and mosquitos have no purpose. They are G-d's messengers showing that the weak can overcome the mighty. . .

---

[17] a small animal that terrifies a lion with its loud cry (Rashi).

GOATS AND SHEEP

SHABBOS 77b

GEMARA: R. Zeira asked R. Yehudah: Why do goats in a herd walk in front of the sheep? R. Yehudah replied: They follow the pattern of the creation of the world. First there was darkness and afterward there was light, so too, [goats which are usually black, go before the sheep which are usually white].

R. Zeira then asked: Why is the hind part of sheep covered [with a broad tail], while goats [have thin tails leaving their hind parts uncovered? The Gemara answers:] The [sheep, the] animal [whose wool we use to cover ourselves] is itself covered; [the goat] the animal whose hair we do not use to cover ourselves, is uncovered.

Biologists explain the anatomy of every creature in nature. The Talmud also explains the purpose of things in nature, for example: why fingers are shaped like pegs, and why the ear is hard but its lobe is soft. However, this Gemara does not seem to fall into this category.

These statements should be understood in a figurative sense. The goats walking in front of the herd, symbolize the Greek empire, which is compared to a goat, as it says, [referring to the Greeks], *Then the he-goat grew greatly* (Daniel 8;8). Yisrael is compared to sheep, as it says, *Yisrael is like scattered sheep* (Yirmeyah 50:17).

During the era of the second Beis Hamikdash there were no
Jewish kings until the rise of the Chashmona'im (Hasmonean) dy-
nasty and Hordus (Herod). They came to power many centuries
after the rule of Alexander the Great and other Greek monarchs.

R. Zeira was asking: Why did the Greek empire—the goat—
march in front, reigning during the time of the second Beis
Hamikdash, long before the sheep—the Jewish kings—governed?

R. Yehudah replied: This follows the pattern of the creation of
the world. First there was darkness, as it says, *With darkness on the
face of the depths* (Bereishis 1:2), and then light, as it says, *Let there
be light* (1:3). The Midrash expounds: *Darkness on the face of the
depths*—that is Greece, for they darkened the eyes of Yisrael [with
their evil decrees]. The Greeks were overthrown by the Chashmona'im, who are represented by light, for they rose to power after
the miracle of the Chanukah lights.

Revealed and Hidden Sins

R. Zeira's question: Why is the hind part of sheep covered [with a
broad tail], while the hind parts of goats are uncovered?, can be explained with the following Gemara: The sin of the earlier generation [of the first Beis Hamikdash—symbolized by the goat], was
done openly, [for they did not hide their wrongdoing], therefore,
the time of their redemption [at the end of the Babylonian exile]
was revealed to them.[18] By contrast, the sin of the ["sheep"] the
later generations [of the second Beis Hamikdash], was not revealed, [for their baseless hatred was hidden in their heart].
Therefore, the time of their redemption was never revealed, [and
we do not know when our exile will end] (Yoma 9b).

---

[18] *When Babylon's seventy years are over . . . I will fulfill My promise and bring you
back to that place* (*Yirmeyah* 29:10).

Camels and Oxen

SHABBOS 77b

> [The GEMARA continues: R. Zeira asked] Why do camels have short tails? [R. Yehudah answered]: Because they eat thorns, [and were they to have long tail, they would get caught in the thorns (Rashi)]. Why do oxen have long tails?—Because they graze in pastures, and need to chase away the flies.

The Gemara says: The Holy One, blessed be He, said: I do not judge Yisrael the way I judge idol worshippers. I punish Yisrael piecemeal, a little at a time, as the hen picks at its chicken feed. Compare this to a man who lent money to both his friend and his enemy. He accept payments in small installments from his friend, but demands payment in full from his enemy. [So too, G-d punishes Yisrael bit by bit] (Avodah Zarah 4a).

This Gemara helps us understand R. Zeira's question: Why is a camel's tail short?

The camel represents Babylonia, as the Midrash expounds the verse, *And the camel,* (Vayikra 11:4)—this is the Babylonian empire, for the word *gamel*—camel, can also be translated as retribution and it says Hashem will take retribution from Babylon.

A tail is a symbol of lowliness and downfall. The camel's short tail signifies the sudden collapse of Babylonia, with its fall from the pinnacle of power to the depth of defeat. As it says, *King Belshatzar made a great feast* (Daniel 5:1) [at the peak of his reign], and the chapter ends, *That very night Belshatzar was slain. Then Daryavesh (Darius) the Mede received the kingship* (Daniel 5:30, 6:1). Thus Babylonia's retribution came precipitously, with a one-time, "payment in full."

R. Yehudah answered: Camels have short tails, because they eat thorns. [The Babylonians, who are compared to camels, destroyed the Beis Hamikdash,] and many tzaddikim, as it says, *For they have devoured Yaakov, and destroyed his habitation* (Tehillim 79:7). Eating thorns refers to the destruction of the tzadikim as we find in the Gemara: Disaster comes to the world when there are wicked people in it. Their first victims are tzaddikim, as it says, *If a fire gets out of control and spreads through the thorns and a stack of grain was consumed* (Shemos 22:5). When is a fire uncontrollable? Only when there are thorns nearby (Bava Kamma 60a). The tzaddikim are always their first victims, for [the "stack of grain" symbolizes the tzaddikim]. [To sum up:] Because of their wickedness, the reign of the Babylonian empire was cut short.

R. Zeira then asked: Why does an ox have a long tail? The ox symbolizes the kingdom of Yisrael, as we find Yosef being called: *The first-born of his ox* (Devarim 33:17). R. Zeira was asking: Why is Yisrael's humiliation drawn out? Since they too worshipped idols, [should they not have been punished in full immediately?] Rav Yehudah answered: Because the ox lives in a pasture, it needs his long tail to chase away the flies. The flies stand for sins as it says, *Dead flies putrefy the perfumer's oil* (Koheles 10:1). G-d does not allow Yisrael's sins to join together, rather He punishes them a little at a time [so as not to destroy them]. Therefore the *galus* lasts so long].

THE SOFT FEELERS OF THE LOCUST

SHABBOS 77b

[The GEMARA continues: R. Zeira asked:] Why are the feelers of a locust soft? Because they live among the willow trees, and if they had hard feelers they would break against the trees, causing the

locust to go blind. As Shmuel said: If you want to
blind a locust, tear its feelers.

Yisrael in exile is compared to weak creatures like locusts or
worms whose only power lay in their mouth [with which
they devour vegetation. So too, Yisroel's power is only through
prayer]. R. Zeira asked: Why are the feelers of a locust soft?
Meaning, why are the Jews submissive despite the fact that they
have some autonomy in exile, represented by the feelers? Rav
Yehudah answered: The Jews in exile among the willows, which al-
lude to wicked governments, are subservient, because one should
always be gentle and flexible like a reed [in his relationship with
others] and never hard and unyielding like a cedar tree. Were the
Jews to be tough and arrogant, they would be expelled from place
to place, with their very existence at risk. They would become
[spiritually] blind, unable to see the bright future.

TWO CROWNS

SHABBOS 88a

GEMARA: When B'nei Yisrael said: *We will do*, before *We will hear*, (Shemos 24:7), 600,000 angels
came and placed two crowns [of Divine radiance]
on the head of every Jew, one for, *We will do,* and
one for, *We will hear.* But when they sinned
[through the golden calf], 1,200,000 angels of
destruction came down and took away their
crowns, as it says, *The people took off the ornaments
that they had on from Mount Chorev* (33:6). . .

Rabbi Yochanan said, Moshe merited and received all [the crowns] . . .

Raish Lakish said: In time to come, the Holy One, blessed be He, will give them back, never again to remove them, as it says, *Then the redeemed of Hashem will return and come to Tzion with glad song, with eternal gladness on their heads. They will attain joy and gladness, and sadness and sighing will flee* (Yeshayah 35:10).

When they accepted the crown of Torah, they were rewarded with the two crowns of *malchus*—kingship—and *kehunah*—priesthood. As Hashem said at the Giving of the Torah, *You will be to Me a kingdom of priests* (Shemos 19:6), signifying the crowns of kingship and priesthood.

With their statement, they accepted the two [types of commandments] of the Torah. "We will do," means accepting the positive commandments. "We will hear," means accepting the negative commandments.

Each of the 600,000 angels carried two crowns. In his right hand, as reward for accepting the positive commandments, he held the crown of priesthood, which represents the Divine attribute of *Chesed*—Kindness and Compassion. In his left hand, as reward for accepting the negative commandments, was the crown of kingship, which represents the divine attribute of *Din*—Justice.

The Crowns Are Taken Away

The Gemara says: When they sinned with the golden calf, transgressing the positive commandment of *I am Hashem your G-d*, and the negative commandment of *Do not have any other gods before Me* (Shemos 20:2,3), which were commandments they heard directly from G-d, 1,200,000 angels of destruction took away the two crowns. However, the crowns were not actually removed [immediately]. G-d agreed to delay full punishment at that time, declaring that they would suffer some of the punishment for the sin of the *eigel* whenever they would sin in the future, as it says, *On the day*

that *I will make My account I will take this sin of theirs into account*
(Shemos 32:34)[19]. The Gemara says that this came true at the de-
struction of the Beis Hamikdash, as it says, *[Hashem called
Yechezkel,] saying, "Bring near those appointed over the city"*
(Yechezkel 9:2) (Sanhedrin 102a).

[At the destruction of the Beis Hamikdash] both priesthood and
kingship came to an end, as it says, *The two olives* [i.e., the priesthood of Aharon and the kingship of David] *that were eliminated
will shine again in the locked garden.* (Shir Hashirim *4:12)*

[The removal of the crowns at the destruction of the Beis
Hamikdash is also indicated in the verse,] *Thus says Hashem,
Elokim: Remove the turban, lift off the crown!* (Yechezkel 21:31)
which refers to the loss of priesthood and kingship.

The deeper meaning of the verse, *The people took off the ornaments that they had on from Mount Chorev* (Shemos 33:6) is, that
they lost their ornaments—the crowns of priesthood and kingship
at the destruction of the Beis Hamikdash. Mount Chorev refers to
the destruction of the Beis Hamikdash, because Mount refers to
the Bais Hamikdash, and *chorev* means, destruction.

1,200,000 angels removed the crowns [which is twice the number of angels that installed the crowns], because they lost the
crowns twice: at the destruction of both the first and the second
Beis Hamikdash.

Moshe merited these crowns, because both the crown of priesthood and kingship, are subordinate to the crown of Torah. Surely
no one was greater than Moshe in Torah which is called by his
name, *Toras Moshe*, therefore he became king and served as kohein
during the seven day inaugural period of the Mishkan.

Indeed, immediately following the verse, *The people took off the
ornaments* it says, *Moshe took the tent* (33:7), meaning, the tent of
Torah, thereby meriting the crowns of priesthood and kingship as
well. They were never taken away from him.

---

[19] In this verse Hashem says that He will one day punish the Jews for the sin of the
golden calf. Maharsha says that the Gemara refers to the 17th of Tammuz, the day
on which Moshe saw the *eigel* and smashed the *Luchos*. Numerous tragedies oc-
curred on that day.

The Crowns Will Be Returned

Although the two crowns were taken away from the Jews at the destruction of the Beis Hamikdash, in time to come, the Holy One, blessed be He, will give them back, never again to remove them, as it says, *Then the redeemed of Hashem will return and come to Tzion with glad song, with eternal gladness on their heads. They will attain joy and gladness, and sadness and sighing will flee* (Yeshayah 35:10). This will come to pass at the final redemption which will be brought about by Hashem—not by an angel, as was the case in the earthly redemption about which it says, *An angel before Him saved them* (Yeshayah 63:9). [About the ultimate redemption] it says, *with eternal gladness on their heads* (Yeshayah 35:10) referring to the two crowns, which will endure forever.

THE SECRET OF THE ANGELS

SHABBOS 88a

GEMARA: When B'nei Yisrael said *We will do*, before *We will hear*, a heavenly voice went forth and said: "Who revealed to My children this secret that is used by the ministering angels?" As it says, *Bless G-d, O His angels, mighty creatures who do His bidding, who listen to the voice of His word* (Tehillim 103:20).

[**S**aying *We will do*, before *We will hear*,] holds a mystery [known only to angels]. An angel is a spiritual being whose mind is focused exclusively on doing G-d's will. The moment an angel wishes to do something, it is as if it is done. By contrast, man, being a composite of body and soul, has to contend with the *yetzer* *hara*, the evil impulse. Therefore, man is not unconditionally willing to obey his Father in Heaven because his *yetzer hara* tempts him to transgress.

However at the Giving of the Torah this secret [of the angels] was revealed to the Jews, for at that moment they were like angels, totally committed to do the will of their Father in Heaven, as it says, *G-d said to Moshe: "If only their hearts would always remain this way"* (Devarim 5:26). G-d wished that the two parts of their hearts—the good and the bad impulse—should remain as one mind, like the angels who unreservedly do G-d's bidding, even before hearing His command.

Dialogue With the Angels

shabbos 88b

GEMARA: [When Moshe went up to heaven to receive the Torah] the ministering angels said to G-d: "Do You want to give this cherished treasure that has been hidden by You for 974 generations before the creation of the world, to one who is nothing but flesh and blood? *What is man that You are mindful of him, mortal man that You take note of him!* . . . *It is only right that Your glory should be conferred on heaven* (Tehillim 8:5)."

The angels calling the Torah a hidden treasure, were referring to its mystical portions. Therefore they said, *It is only right that Your glory should be conferred on heaven,* meaning, the mysteries of the Torah should remain in heaven, not given to [man on] earth. Just as the Torah was not given for 974 generations before Creation, and for 26 generations after Creation, because people were not worthy, they are still not worthy, for being born of woman, man is steeped in physicality, unfit to delve into mysticism.

The angels were told: *Out of the mouth of babes and sucklings You have established strength* (Tehillim 8:3). The Gemara explains: The world endures only because of the breath of schoolchildren, for you cannot compare breath that has been tarnished by sin to breath that has not been blemished by sin (Shabbos 119b).

In other words: Although the adults are not worthy of receiving the Torah, the Torah was given because of the schoolchildren, whose breath is not tainted by sin.

Not only did the giving of the Torah to Yisrael ensure the existence of the lower world, it also established the continued existence of the middle world [of stars and planets], as it says in the next verse, *When I behold Your heavens, the work of Your fingers, the moon and the stars that You have set in place* (Tehillim 8:4), for their existence depends on Torah learning as it says, *Were it not for My covenant night and day I would not have set up the laws of heaven and earth* (Yirmeyah 33:25).

MOSHE'S CONVINCING ARGUMENT

SHABBOS 88b

[The angels continued to object, saying:] *What is man [enosh] that You are mindful of him, mortal man [ben adam] that You take note of him* (Tehillim 8:5).

According to this Gemara, the angels said this verse to dissuade G-d from giving the Torah to Moshe]. However, the Gemara in *Sanhedrin* (38b) says the angels raised this protest when G-d wanted to create man.

Because the verse says, *You are mindful,* and *You take note,* using two expressions, it is referring to two protests. Before the creation of man, the angels said, *What is man* [enosh] *that You are mindful of him.* [Man is referred to here as *enosh*], because he was not called *adam* until after his creation, as it says, *He called their name Adam on the day they were created* (Bereishis 5:2).

[The second part of the verse:] *Mortal man* [ben adam] *that you take note of him,* was said when G-d wanted to give the Torah, for at this point the Jews were already called *ben adam, "mortal man."* Indeed, the Gemara says: As compensation for the fact that the angels [contemptuously] called [Moshe] a mere mortal [who is not fit to receive the Torah], he received gifts (Shabbos 89a).

The angels then said, *You have made him but slightly less than the Elokim* (Tehillim 8:6), by revealing the mysteries of the Torah to man. As the Gemara says: Forty-nine [of the fifty] gates of understanding were revealed to Moshe (Rosh Hashanah 21b).

[They continued:] *And You crowned him with honor and splendor,* referring to the crowns of priesthood and kingship, which were given at Sinai.

[Complained the angels:] However B'nei Yisrael are not worthy of this, for they are born from a physical woman and are not fit to receive the mystical aspects of the Torah, which are spiritual. You should rather *Give Your splendor,* the mystical part of the Torah, *to the heavenly beings,* namely the angels, who are qualified to receive mystical teachings.

Hashem told Moshe: "Respond to them."

"Master of the universe," replied Moshe, "I am afraid they may consume me with their fiery breath," meaning: I am afraid they will defeat me with the breath of their mouth which is purely spiritual, and therefore more capable of understanding mysticism than man who is steeped in physical matter. Alternatively, we can explain he was afraid the angels would defeat him because they are free of sin, as opposed to man who sins.

Hashem answered: "Hold on to My Throne of Glory, and give them an answer," meaning, although man has a physical body, nevertheless, since the souls of the tzaddikim are bound in the

Bond of Life underneath the Throne of Glory, he is capable of understanding spiritual concepts and abstract mystical thoughts.

Bolstered by G-d's assurance that man is capable of comprehending the mystical level of the Torah, Moshe argued that the Torah should, in fact, be given to him rather than to the angels in heaven, because the angels cannot fulfill the physical aspects of the Torah.

Turning to the angels he said: It says in the Torah: *I am Hashem your G-d who brought you out of Egypt* (Shemos 20:2). "Did you go down to Egypt? Were you slaves to Pharaoh?"

This point is indicated in the next verse of our psalm, *You gave [man] dominion over Your handiwork. You placed everything under his feet, sheep and cattle, all of them, even the beasts of the field* (Tehillim 8:7). This parallels the verse, *They shall rule over the fish of the sea, the birds of the sky . . .* (Bereishis 1:28).

[Moshe argued:] If You don't give the Torah to B'nei Yisrael, they will not be able to eat fish, meat or fowl, for the Gemara says, One ignorant of Torah may not eat the flesh of cattle (Pesachim 49b). However by virtue of their soul, which enables them to receive the Torah and the mitzvos they can rule over everything [and eat fish, meat, or fowl].

Immediately, the angels admitted that it was proper for Hashem to give the Torah to Yisrael, for the physical aspects of the Torah do not apply in heaven. Therefore the psalm concludes, *Hashem, our Master, how mighty is Your Name throughout the earth!* (Tehillim 8:10), and does not mention, *Let Your glory be conferred on heaven*, because the plain meaning of the Torah applies in this world and not in heaven.

When the angels heard G-d declare that by virtue of man's soul and intellect he is capable of receiving the mystical interpretation of the Torah, each angel befriended Moshe and revealed a secret to him.

This is the meaning of the verse, *You went up to the heights, you have taken captives, you took gifts* (Tehillim 68:19). Taking captives, refers to the plain meaning of the Torah, which was like a captive in heaven, for it does not apply to angels, as Moshe contended.

You took gifts refers to the secrets of the Torah which were given to Moshe by the angels.

Even the Angel of Death, the primary accusing angel, gave him a gift, confiding his secret to him [that incense can check a plague]. For it says, *He put on the incense, and made an atonement for the people . . . and the plague was checked* (Bamidbar 17:12,13). Rashi explains, the Torah does not say, incense can stop a plague, thus Moshe must have heard it from the Angel of Death.

Though many things are not expressly commanded in the Torah, rather we derive from the narrative what Hashem commanded Moshe to do, in this case, it is not likely that G-d commanded Moshe to present incense to make an atonement, for in the previous verse G-d says, *Stand clear of this community, and I will destroy them in an instant* (17:10). Therefore, we must conclude that Moshe was taught this by the Angel of Death.

THE INVERTED LETTERS *NUN*

SHABBOS 115b

> GEMARA: *When the Ark went forth, Moshe said, "Arise, O Hashem, and scatter Your enemies! Let Your foes flee before You!" When it came to rest, it says, "Return, O Hashem, to the myriads of Yisrael's thousands"* (Bamidbar 10:35,36). The Holy One, blessed be He, inserted signs [in the Torah] before and after these verses, to indicate that this is not the proper place for this section. Rebbi says, this is not the reason, rather to indicate that this is a book of its own.

According to the first opinion, inverted *nun*s are inserted in the Torah text before and after these verses, to demonstrate that this is not the proper place for this section. Rather these verses were placed here to make a break between [the] evil [mentioned in the preceding section] and the evil [mentioned int he following section]. Inverted *nuns* were chosen, because *nun*, the first letter of the word *nafal*, "to fall" suggests, "downfall." This is the reason *Ashrei* has no verse beginning with a *nun*. By inverting the *nuns* they are converted to a good omen, demonstrating that Yisrael's downfall will be overturned into goodness, growth, and advance. In fact the next verse in *Ashrei* says, *Hashem will support the fallen* [nofelim] (Tehillim 145:14).

According to Rebbi, these verses were set apart, to indicate that this section counts as a separate book, as it says, *Wisdom has carved out her seven pillars* (Mishlei 9:1). *Nun*s were used, to tell us that although it is a small book, it too contains the fifty gates of understanding.[20] The *nun*s are upended to indicate [that the fifty gates] are beyond human comprehension. Even Moshe whose name is mentioned in these two verses could grasp only forty-nine of the fifty gates of understanding.

The Torah is divided into seven books, hinting that it was Hashem's nursling at the seven days of Creation, as it says, *I [the Torah] was then His nursling* (Mishlei 8:30), and, *He has carved out her seven pillars* (Mishlei 9:1), for the seven books of the Torah are the blueprint of the seven days of Creation.

SAVED FROM THREE CALAMITIES

SHABBOS 118a

GEMARA: One who eats three meals on Shabbos is saved from three calamities: The pangs of Mashiach, the suffering of Gehinnom, and the war of Gog and Magog. We derive that he will be

---

[20] The numeric value of *nun* is 50.

saved from the pangs of Mashiach for concerning Shabbos it says "day" and concerning the pangs of Mashiach it says *Behold, I send you Eliyahu the prophet before the coming of the great and awesome day of Hashem* (Malachi 3:23).

Rashi explains that the pangs of Mashiach will occur before the coming of Mashiach, however the verse cited in the Gemara as proof, *Behold, I send you Eliyahu the prophet before the coming of the great and awesome day of Hashem* (Malachi 3:23), refers to the day Mashiach actually comes. Perhaps the Gemara is bringing proof that one who eats three meals on Shabbos will be saved from the pangs of Mashiach thereby living to see the coming of Mashiach.

After these three catastrophic periods, will come the time of ultimate tranquility for tzaddikim, symbolized by the Shabbos. Therefore it is only fitting that one who delights in the Shabbos now, which corresponds to the time of tranquility following the periods of affliction, should be saved from the three periods of affliction, and instead they should be days of serenity and peace.

A BOUNDLESS INHERITANCE

SHABBOS 118a

Someone who takes delight in the Shabbos is given a boundless inheritance, for it says, *Then [in the days of Mashiach] you will indulge in spiritual pleasures, I will set you astride the heights of the earth, and let you enjoy the heritage of your father Yaakov* (Yeshayah 58:14).

The Beis Yosef in Tur Orach Chaim section 242, explains that this reward is measure for measure. Since he spends without limit for the enjoyment of Shabbos, he is given a boundless inheritance.

Another explanation: Taking delight in Shabbos affects one spiritually, for it feeds his *neshamah yeseirah*—additional soul—granting it life in the World to Come, a time of complete Shabbos[21], which is not bound by physical boundaries, therefore, the reward for taking delight in Shabbos is boundless. . .

The boundless blessing [of Shabbos] is considered the blessing of Yaakov rather than the blessing of Avraham or Yitzchak, because included in their inheritance were certain territories which were assigned to the children of Lot and Eisav, as it says, *To the children of Lot have I given Ar as an inheritance . . . the children of Eisav who dwell in Se'ir* (Devarim 2:8,9). These territories were out of Eretz Yisroel and are indeed bounded. However, Yaakov, the third of the patriarchs, was able to bequeath to his children, the additional *berachah* of "an unrestricted, boundless [spiritual] inheritance."

THE REWARD FOR A MITZVAH

SHABBOS 118b

Rav Nachman said: I am deserving, because I fulfilled the mitzvah of three meals on Shabbos.

Rashi translates the expression "I am deserving" to mean, "May I be rewarded [for fulfilling the mitzvah]." This translation is open to question, for one should not seek a reward

---

[21] an allusion to the World to Come after the final redemption.

for doing a mitzvah. As the Mishnah says: Don't be like servants who serve their master for the sake of receiving a reward; instead be like servants who serve their master not for the sake of receiving a reward (Avos 1:3).

Rav Nachman's word may be explained as follows. We are taught, "[Heaven] guides a person along the way he wants to follow" (Makkos 10b), and, "One who comes to cleanse himself, is helped [by Heaven]" (Shabbos 104a), meaning, G-d helps one carry out his good intentions. Rav Nachman meant: Because I fulfilled the mitzvah of having three meals on Shabbos, Heaven will help me continue fulfilling this mitzvah.

In the same vein, the Gemara says: Whereby do the wealthy merit wealth? [They are blessed] because they [use their wealth to] honor Shabbos (Shabbos 119a)[22].

Similarly, Rav Yehudah said: For being engrossed in my prayer I deserve a reward from Heaven that I continue to pray with deep intent.

Indeed whenever the Gemara quotes someone as saying I am deserving, he means: "Since I am determined to fulfill this mitzvah to perfection, may Heaven help me carry out my intention."

THE SIGNIFICANCE OF THE NUMBER THIRTEEN

꞊꞊◗꞊꞊

SHABBOS 119a

GEMARA: Yosef-Who-Honored-Shabbos bought [a fish]. When he opened it he found a jewel, which he sold for thirteen roomfuls of gold dinarim.

---

[22] As it says, *It is the blessing of Hashem that enriches* (*Mishlei* 10:22). The Midrash says that this refers to Shabbos (*Midrash Rabbah, Bereishis* 74).

Rashi says this is an exaggeration; indeed the number thirteen is often used to denote a large number. However, it is difficult to understand why thirteen should be used as a figure of speech, for thirteen is not in the set of tens or hundreds like the number sixty which is often used to signify a large number.

It seems the number thirteen was chosen because it relates to concepts of *kedushah*—holiness, such as the "thirteen Divine attributes." Furthermore, the *gematria* (numeric value) of *echad* (one) equals thirteen (*alef*=1;*ches*=8;*daled*=4). Thus the number one, alludes to the thirteen attributes which reflect G-d's Oneness. The 13 attributes themselves are not separate entities, except for the way they affect the beneficiary of those attributes.

Moreover, [the fact that 13 relates to *kedushah* is evident] in the thirteen rules through which the Torah is expounded. Additionally, a boy of thirteen year takes on the sanctity of mitzvos.

For this reason, Rabbi Abba bought meat [in honor of Shabbos] for thirteen [half-zuz] coins from thirteen butchers. Probably, Yosef-who-honored Shabbos, also bought his Shabbos food in units of thirteen and was therefore rewarded with thirteen roomfuls of gold *dinarim*.

The Gemara relates that Shmuel sent [Rabbi Yochanan] thirteen camel loads[23] of questions concerning forbidden foods (Chullin 93b). [His questions certainly] were matters dealing with *kedushah*. So too, the Gemara relates that G-d granted Rabbi Elazar ben Pedas thirteen rivers of balsam oil as clear as the Euphrates and the Tigris, to enjoy in the World to Come, for the atmosphere of the World to Come is one of *kedushah*.

---

[23] according to others, parchment scrolls.

A SAVORY SPICE CALLED SHABBOS

===((()))===

SHABBOS 119a

GEMARA: The Roman emperor [Hadrian] said to Rabbi Yehoshua ben Chananiah: "Why does the food you prepare for the Sabbath taste so good?" Rabbi Yehoshua replied: "We have a special spice we put into it, and its name is Shabbos." "Give me some of it," the emperor demanded. "It works for those who observe the Sabbath, but it has no effect on people who do not observe the Sabbath," replied Rabbi Yehoshua ben Chananiah.

Indeed there is an actual spice called Shabbos, as we find in the Mishnah. Rabbi Yehoshua actually meant that the Shabbos day gives food a good flavor, however he hoped the emperor would think he was referring to Shabbos the savory herb.

Thinking it was a tasty ingredient, the emperor demanded: "Give me some of it." At this point Rabbi Yehoshua was forced to admit his real intention and said; "It works for those who observe the Sabbath, but it has no effect on those who do not observe the Sabbath".

THE WISHES OF THE TWO ANGELS

===((()))===

SHABBOS 119b

GEMARA: Two ministering angels, one good and the other evil, escort a person on Friday night from the synagogue to his house. When [they] come home to find the candles lit, the table set, and the bed made, the good angel declares: "May the coming Shabbos be just like the present one." The evil angel has no choice but to answer "Amen." But if they do not find [the candles lit, the table set, nor the bed made,] the evil angel wishes: May it be like this the next Shabbos. The good angel has no option but to answer "Amen."

Two angels are appointed for each mitzvah of the Torah, an angel "from the right side" who spurs a person to do the mitzvah, and an angel "from the left side" who entices him to violate the mitzvah. The two angels mentioned in this Gemara are the ones appointed for the mitzvah of Shabbos.

When a person observes the Shabbos properly the good angel says: "May the coming Shabbos be just like the present one," to which the evil angel is forced to respond "Amen." [The evil angel's] answer of "Amen" carries more weight [than the good angel's wish], for we have a rule that, "the admission of the litigant is as a hundred witnesses." Conversely, and for the same reason, the good angel's reluctant response of "Amen" carries more weight than the evil angel's wish.

BABYLON AND ROME, THE TWO DESTROYERS

SHABBOS 150a

GEMARA: [Nevuchadnetzar said:] *Additional greatness was given to me* (Daniel 4:33). This teaches that [Nevuchadnetzar] rode on a male lion and on his head he tied a snake, in fulfillment of the verse, *I have even delivered the beast of the field to [Nevuchadnetzar] to serve him* (Yirmeyah 27:6).

Rashi explains that the snake was tied to the head of the lion. Another interpretation is that Nevuchadnetzar tied the snake to his own head as a crown. He rode on a lion because the Lion (Leo) was Nevuchadnetzar's sign of the zodiac, as it says [about Nevuchadnetzar], *The lion has left his den; the destroyer of nations has set out* (Yirmeyah 4:7). For this reason the Beis Hamikdash was destroyed in Av, the month under the zodiacal sign of the Lion (Leo).

The snake on [Nevuchadnetzar's] head alludes to the primordial Serpent which is the source of Eisav's (Rome's) power at whose hands the second Beis Hamikdash was destroyed.

We wrote earlier that the destruction of the two Batei Mikdash was really one event, beginning with the destruction of the first Beis Hamikdash by Nevuchadnetzar, and ending with the destruction of the second Beis Hamikdash by [the Romans] who are the descendants of Eisav.

Therefore, the future downfall [of Babylon and Edom (Rome)] is mentioned jointly in the passage, *Remember, Hashem, for the offspring of Edom, the day of Yerushalayim . . . O violated daughter of Babylon, praiseworthy is he who repays you in accordance with the manner that you treated us. Praiseworthy is he who will clutch and dash your infants against the rock* (Tehillim 137:7-9).

TZADDIKIM LIVE ON AFTER DEATH

SHABBOS 152b

GEMARA: Rav Mari said: Even the tzaddikim will ultimately return to dust, as it says, *And the dust returns to the ground as it was* (Koheles 12:7).

Diggers were once digging Rav Nachman's land, and hit Rav Achai ben Yoshia, [who unbeknownst to them, was buried there], and he growled. Reporting this to Rav Nachman, he went there and asked: "Who are you?" Came the reply: "I am Achai ben Yoshia." Said Rav Nachman: ["Why is your body still intact?] Didn't Rav Mari say: 'Even the tzaddikim will ultimately return to dust?'" Rav Achai bar Yoshia retorted, "Who is this Mari? I never heard of him." Said Rav Nachman: "But [his statement is verified] as it says, '*And the dust returns to the ground as it was*' (Koheles 12:7)'"! Rav Achai ben Yoshia replied: ". . . It says, *Envy causes the bones to rot* (Mishlei 14:30), thus one who was never envious, will not rot."

Rav Nachman then poked Rav Achai bar Yoshia and saw that his body had substance. . . . Said Rav Nachman: "But it says, *You are dust and to dust you will return* (Bereishis 3:19). Replied Rav Achai ben Yoshia: "This verse refers to one minute before the Revival of the Dead [when even the tzaddikim will turn to dust, but they will immediately return to life again]."

Why didn't Rav Nachman mention the Torah verse, *You are dust and to dust you will return*, first, instead of citing the verse from *Koheles, And the dust returns to the ground as it was.*

Furthermore: Why did Rav Achai bar Yoshia initially dismiss Rav Mari's statement [that tzaddikim will return to dust]? Why didn't he answer that Rav Mari was also speaking about one minute before the Resurrection?

Thirdly: Why does it say: Rav Nachman saw Rav Achai's body had substance [after poking it]? He knew there was substance in him, for he asked him, "Doesn't it say, *And the dust returns to the ground as it was,*" implying that his body was still intact.

The Gemara says: There are three partners in [the creation of] man: his father, his mother, and the Holy One, blessed be He. His father supplies the bones and sinews; his mother provides the flesh and blood; and the Holy One, blessed be He, gives him the spirit and soul (Niddah 31a). Because of these elementary components, a man's character has three aspects that may be either good or bad: He is either good to G-d, good to his fellowman, and good to himself, or conversely, he is bad to G-d, bad to his fellowman, and bad to himself. His attitude toward G-d stems from his soul; his attitude toward his fellowman stems from his mother who provides his flesh and blood. His posture toward himself [*atzmo*] stems from his father who supplies his bones [*atzamos*]. Two of man's components survive after death: (1) man's soul which comes from G-d [which is immortal], and (2) one of the bones which he receives from his father remains intact after death; [this bone is the nucleus] from which he is revived at the Resurrection.

In this connection we can understand the Gemara which says: When a tzaddik leaves this world, three groups of ministering angels welcome him. But when a wicked man perishes from the world, three groups of angels of destruction meet him (Kesubos 104a).

It is well-known, that an angel is created from every action a person does, whether good or bad, as our sages say: If one does a mitzvah he acquires an advocate for himself. Therefore, when a tzaddik whose soul lives on, departs from this world, three groups of angels that were created from the three types of mitzvos he performed, by being good to G-d, good to his fellowman, and good to himself, greet him. One group declares, *He will come in peace,* (Yeshayah 57:2), because he lived in peace and kindness with his fellowmen. Another group says, *He walks in integrity* (ibid.) because he was good to himself. A third group says, *They will rest on their resting places* (ibid.) referring to his soul, which being encased in his body, had no rest in this world.

Conversely the Gemara says: When a wicked man is destroyed— for the death of the wicked is indeed their destruction—three groups of angels of destruction greet him. One group declares,

"There is no peace for the wicked," said Hashem (Yeshayah 48:22), because he treated people badly and did not have pleasant relations with them. Another group says, *that you should die in sorrow* (Yeshayah 50:11) because he was bad to himself. The third group says, *Descend and be laid to rest with the uncircumcised* (Yechezkel 32:19). Because he was bad toward heaven, he must rest with the uncircumcised who are not admitted to the World to Come.

[Rav Achai bar Yoshia] dismissed Rav Mari's teaching, thinking he meant that tzaddikim will return to dust completely, with no bones remaining and only the Divine soul remaining after death.

After Rav Nachman mentioned the verse that even the bones will return to dust, Rav Achai explained that this only refers to the envious, who are bad towards themselves, however the bones of the righteous will remain.

Rav Nachman was prompted to say he had substance, when he saw that not only were his bones intact but even his flesh which comes from the mother was intact. He asked, "Doesn't it say, *You are dust and to dust you will return* (Bereishis 3:19) about the flesh? Rav Achai replied that this refers to one minute before the resurrection.

MESECHTA ERUVIN

A Warning for Scribes

GEMARA: We learnt in a Braisa: Rebbi Meir said, ". . . when I came to Rabbi Yishmael, he asked, 'My son, what is your occupation?' I answered, 'I am a [Torah] scribe.' He replied, 'Be painstaking, because your work is Heavenly work. If you omit or add even a single letter, you will destroy the entire universe.' "

Tosafos explains that one can commit blasphemy by adding a letter to the Torah. [For example,] When writing *Bereishis bara* ["In the beginning G-d created"], if one adds the letter *vav* to the word *bara*, writing instead, *Bereishis bare'u*, [he changes the meaning from "In the beginning G-d created," to "In the beginning they created."] Thus he denies the Oneness of G-d and commits blasphemy.

Tosafos does not elaborate about omitting a letter, however Kabbalah teaches that the entire Torah is comprised of Names of G-d. With the letters of the Torah, G-d created and sustains the world. Therefore, by omitting a letter, one alters the Names of G-d which sustain the world, thereby destroying it.

Good and Bad Character Traits

GEMARA: G-d raises whoever humbles himself, and lowers whoever exalts himself. Greatness runs from whoever seeks it, and pursues whoever shuns it. One who "forces the hour" [exerting himself in a futile attempt to succeed,] will find that his efforts bring disaster in its wake.

At first glance these three cases seem redundant, for each teaches the same lesson.

We know that one must be good toward Heaven, toward his fellow man, and toward himself. Conversely one must not be haughty toward Heaven, toward his fellow man, nor toward himself.

[The first statement refers to one's relationship towards Heaven:] G-d lifts up one who is good toward Heaven and humbles himself before G-d. Conversely, one who exalts himself against G-d is humbled by G-d.

[The next statement refers to one's relationship towards others:] When one acts arrogantly, seeking to dominate his fellow man he loses their respect, as the Gemara says: A haughty person is not even accepted by the members of his own family (Bava Basra 98a). On the other hand, one who shuns greatness, treating people graciously, will be pursued by greatness, and people will favor him.

[Finally the Gemara refers to the relationship between man and himself:] If someone "forces the hour," [exerting himself in a futile attempt to succeed,] his efforts will only bring disaster, as the Gemara says: The position of the sign of the zodiac at a given hour determines a person's destiny, [therefore, one cannot influence his fate]. However, in the merit of not trying to change one's fortune [rather submitting to one's fate,] G-d will have mercy on him changing his luck [for the better], so that the time of day [i.e., his horoscope] favors him. Such was the case with Avraham. The Gemara relates: Avraham exclaimed: "I have looked at my constellation, and find that I am not destined to beget a son." Replied G-d: "Do you think that since [you were born] when Jupiter was in the West [where it is cold, which causes impotence (Rashi), you won't have children]? I will turn Jupiter around and place it in the East."

THE FOUR METHODS OF
EXPOUNDING THE TORAH

———— ══◉══ ————

ERUVIN 21a

GEMARA: It says, *To every goal I have seen an end,
but Your commandment is exceedingly broad
(Tehillim* 119:96). This statement [about the mag-
nitude of the Torah] was made by David, but he
did not elucidate [the exact measurements]. Nor
did Iyov elucidate it, for he said, *Its measure is
longer than the earth and wider than the sea (Iyov*
11:9). Yechezkel did not elucidate it either, for he
said, *He spread it out before me; it was inscribed
within and without, and there was written on it
lamentations, moaning, and woe (Yechezkel* 2:10).
Finally Zechariah came and elucidated it, as it says,
*He said to me: "What do you see?" I answered, "I see
a folded scroll: twenty cubits wide and ten cubits
high" (Zechariah* 5:2). When it is unfolded it will be
twenty cubits by twenty cubits. He also said, *"And
behold it is written front and back."* If the front will
be separated from the back, [and placed alongside
it, it will measure twenty by forty.]

The Torah can be interpreted on four levels:

p'shat — [the plain straightforward meaning of the text];

d'rash — [homiletic, metaphoric interpretation; also an interpretation according to the 13 rules by which the Torah is explained
as enumerated by Rabbi Yishmael in *Sifra*];

remez — philosophical interpretations which refer to the Works
of Creation.

sod — kabbalistic interpretation, dealing with the [mystical] Works of the Divine Chariot [as described in the first chapter of Yechezkel].

The four approaches of interpretation are known by the acronym *pardes* [*pshat, remez, d'rash, sod*].

Commenting on the verse, *Hashem spoke to you face to face* (Devarim 5:4), the Midrash says: [The Hebrew word for face, is *Panim*, which translates literally as "faces"] this refers to two ways of interpreting the Torah, and [the Hebrew word for "to face" which is *befanim*, translates literally as "faces," also] refers to two ways of interpretation. Since *p'shat* and *d'rash* expound the revealed meaning of the Torah and mitzvos, they were paired together under the plural word *panim*. And since *remez* and *sod* deal with the mystical aspects of the Torah, they were grouped under the plural word *befanim*.

David said, *Your commandment is exceedingly broad,* referring only to the revealed part of the Torah, which is the mitzvos.

Iyov spoke about understanding the revealed portions of the Torah in general terms, saying, *Its measure is longer than the earth.* Regarding the performance of mitzvos he merely said, *It is wider than the sea,* for the length is longer than the width, just as the study of Torah is greater than fulfilling the mitzvos. He did not specify that there are four methods of interpretation.

Yechezkel who saw the Torah as *being inscribed within and without,* did not explain the full extent of the Torah. For *within* refers to the revealed aspect of the mitzvos, while *without*—somewhat less revealed—refers to the *d'rash* (homiletic) aspect of the mitzvos. . . .

Finally Zechariah appeared, and he saw all four methods of interpretation. At first he saw a folded scroll representing the *p'shat,* the plain revealed meaning of the Torah. After it unfolded, a second approach was added, that of *d'rash* which is not as revealed as the *p'shat.* The scroll was written front and back, so that when it is split [and the written surfaces are placed side by side], two more parts are added, namely *remez* and *sod*, the mystical interpretations which can be understood only through penetrating analysis, represented by the splitting of the scroll.

This concept [of the four ways of interpretation] is expressed in the verse, *Now if you obey Me and keep My covenant, you shall be My special treasure because all the world is Mine. You shall be a kingdom of priests and a holy nation . . .* (*Shemos* 19:5,6).

If you obey Me, refers to *p'shat.*

And keep My covenant, alludes to d'rash, [which is the Oral Torah], for G-d made His covenant with Yisrael only because of the Oral Torah, as it says, *Since it is through these words that I have made a covenant with you and Yisrael* (*Shemos* 34:27).

You shall be My special treasure, refers to the study of the Works of Creation, for through this, you will come to recognize that *all the world is Mine,* and that I created it.

You shall be a kingdom of priests, refers to grasping the profundity of *sod* and the mystery of the Works of the Divine Chariot.

A SEFER TORAH IS A SAFE INVESTMENT

ERUVIN 64a

GEMARA: What should one who takes possession of the property of a convert [who died without children and thus has no legal heirs] do, to be worthy of keeping the property? Let him buy a sefer Torah with [a portion of the property]. Rav Sheshes said: Even a husband who takes control of his wife's estate [should do the same]. Rava said: Even a man who earned a substantial profit in a business deal [should buy a sefer Torah with a portion of his profit]. Rav Papa said: Even a person who found a [valuable] article [should do the same]. Rav Nachman b. Yitzchak said: Even if he only paid for the writing of a pair of *tefillin* [from part of his profit, his wealth will be protected].

Rav Chanin said: From where do we know [that the performance of a mitzvah protects one's wealth]? It says, *Yisrael made a vow to Hashem, and said: "If you give this nation into our hand, we will destroy them and consecrate their cities [for the Tabernacle]. G-d heard Yisrael's voice, and He allowed them to defeat the Canaanites. Yisrael consecrated the cities [for the Tabernacle.]* (Bamidbar 21:2,3).

The word "even" implies that each of the Sages added to the statement of the preceding Sage. [What does each Sage add?] and, why does the Gemara choose the mitzvah of buying a *sefer Torah* over any other mitzvah? Additionally, why does Rav Chanin adduce proof from the verse in *Bamidbar* (21:2), rather than citing the [better known] verse, *Yaakov made a vow saying, "If G-d will be with me, if he will protect me on the journey that I am taking, if He gives me bread and clothing to wear . . . then I will dedicate myself totally to G-d . . . Of all that You give me, I will set aside a tenth for You* (*Bereishis* 28:20-22)?

[Performing a mitzvah protects one from loss] because it teaches a person not to think he earned his wealth by dint of his ingenuity or diligence, as it says, . . . *nor does bread come to the wise* (*Koheles* 9:11). By setting aside a portion of his windfall for a mitzvah, he shows that everything comes from G-d. Buying a *sefer Torah*, is the safest investment, as the Gemara says: If one has taken a deposit from a child, he should invest it for him. How should he invest it? Rav Chisda said: He should buy a *sefer Torah* with it. Rashi explains, he will profit by learning from it while the principal will remain secure . . . (Bava Basra 52a).

Yaakov who was extremely poor, prayed only for food and clothing which are necessities which everyone may expect to receive from G-d, as it says, *He gives food to all flesh* (*Tehillim* 136:25); this is not dependant on one's exertion. However [when Yisrael vowed: *If You give this [Canaanite] nation into our hand, we will consecrate the booty for the Tabernacle*], they were a large throng, and might have been able to defeat the Canaanites by natural means. Nevertheless, they attributed it to G-d in the belief that everything—including nature — is in G-d's hand. Thus, they used the double expression *im nason tittein*, lit. "If give, You will give, this nation into our hand . . ." implying: *Im nason*—even if You let us defeat them by natural means, making it appear as if there were no higher Power helping us; *tittein*—we know that you are the One who gives the Canaanites into our hand, for everything comes from You. Therefore, *we will consecrate [the booty of war for the Tabernacle]*.

So too, when a person appeals to G-d, the true Helper, he should donate some of his wealth for a mitzvah as a reminder that G-d is the One who granted him all his possessions.

Therefore, when a person takes possession of the property of a convert [who died without Jewish children] he should not think he was lucky, rather he should realize it is a gift from G-d. He should buy a *sefer Torah* as an investment guaranteed by G-d. He eats the fruit by learning it in this world, and the principal—the reward for Torah study—remains intact for him in the World to Come.

Rav Sheshes adds that a husband should buy a *sefer Torah* with a portion of his wife's estate, even though the principal does not belong to him, as he is entitled only to the proceeds. He should buy a *sefer Torah* with the profit G-d grants him meanwhile, in order that the principal should remain intact.

Rava adds that even a person who earned a substantial amount in a business deal, which he may lose eventually, should attribute his windfall to G-d rather than to his brilliant investment strategy. Demonstrating this, he should buy a *sefer Torah*, insuring against loss.

Rav Papa adds: Even someone who found a valuable article by chance and did not pray for it, should attribute his find to G-d and contribute toward the purchase of a *sefer Torah*. . .

THREE CHARACTER TRAITS

—————◉—————

ERUVIN 65b

GEMARA: Rebbi Elai said: One can judge a man's character by his cup, by his purse, and by his anger.

Human personality traits fall into three main categories: One who is good to Heaven; One who is good to others; One who is good to himself.

"His purse" refers to the category of being good to others, and dealing honestly with his fellowman.

"His cup" refers to the category of being good to himself, and remaining cool-headed when drinking wine or liquor.

"His anger" refers to the category of being good to Heaven, and not becoming angry [when provoked], for it says:[24] "Anger is as bad as idol worship."

Another explanation is that [purse, cup, and anger] represent the three things that motivate a person to act. He acts either because something is pleasing, profitable, or morally good.

Accordingly, "His cup," represents one who acts for pleasure to satisfy his desires, such as drinking strong beverages.

"His purse," represents one who acts for profit, seeking to profit through fraudulent business practices.

"His anger," represents one who acts because it is morally good, suppressing his anger, because anger is equal to idolatry, which is morally reprehensible.

Since the Hebrew words for "his cup," "his purse," and "his anger"—*bekoso, bekiso, beka'aso* sound alike and begin with the same letter, they were used as a catch phrase to describe the three character traits.

————————————

24 *Zohar* 1:27b.

GLOSSARY

———⟨◉⟩———

AGGADAH or *AGGADIC DERASHOS* - Homiletic discourses
AVRAHAM - Abraham
B'NEI YISRAEL - Children of Israel
B'RIS - covenant
BAMIDBAR - The Book of Numbers
BEIS HAMIKDASH - Holy Temple
BEN - son of
BERACHAH pl. *BERACHOS* - blessing
BEREISHIS - The Book of Genesis
BIRCHAS HAMAZONE - Grace after meals
BRAISA - a section of the oral law
DEVARIM - The Book of Deuteronomy
DIVREI HAYAMIM - The Book of Chronicles
EICHA - The Book of Lamentations
ELIYAHU - Elijah
ERETZ YISRAEL - The Land of Israel
GALUS - exile
GAN EDEN - the garden of eden
GEMARA - Talmud
HAKADOSH BORUCH HU - The Holy One Blessed is He
HALACHAH pl. *HALACHOS* - law
HASHEM - God
KIDDUSH - a declaration sanctifying the beginning of a holy day
KOHEIN - Priest, descendant of Aaron
KOHELES - Ecclesiastes
MASHIACH - The Messiah
MELACHIM - The Book of Kings
MESECHES, MESECHTA - the tractate of
MINCHA - the afternoon prayer
MISHKAN - The Tabernacle
MISHLEI - Proverbs

MISHNAH - compilation of the oral tradition; it also refers to one
    paragraph of this compilation
MITZVAH pl. *MITZVOS* - commandment
PARASHAS, PARSHIOS - the portion [of the Torah]
ROSH HASHANAH - The New Year
RUACH HAKODESH - Divine Inspiration
SEFIROS - emmanations
SHACHARIS - the morning prayer
SHECHINAH - Divine Presence
SHEMA - the portion of the Torah containing the declaration of
    Hashem's unity that we say morning and evening.
SHEMONEH ESREI - the eighteen beracha prayer that we say
    thrice each day
SHEMOS - The Book of Exodus
SHEMUEL - The Book of Samuel
SHIR HASHIRIM - Song of Songs
SHUL - synagogue
TANACH - Scriptures
TEFILLAH, pl. *TEFILLOS* - prayer
TEFILLIN - phylacteries
TEHILLIM - Psalms
TZADDIK pl. *TZADDIKIM* - Pious Person
TZITZIS - fringes worn on a four cornered garment
VAYIKRA - The Book of Leviticus
YECHEZKEL - Ezekiel
YEHOSHUA - Joshua
YERUSHALAYIM - Jerusalem
YESHAYAH - Isaiah
YETZER HARA - evil inclination
YIRMIYAH - Jeremiah
YISRAEL - Israel